Praise for *The Coronation*

"Charles Eisenstein is one of those courageous dissidents who also holds the faith that people can return to love after a hiatus of hate. As we go deeper into this new era of permacrisis, Charles's writings will become ever more pertinent."

—**PROFESSOR JEM BENDELL**, founder and former coordinator, Deep Adaptation Forum

"Charles Eisenstein has taken on the hardest task in the world—writing an intelligent, compassionate, and uncompromising book on the Covid-19 pandemic, without falling into either partisan hysteria or a shameless defense of power. This is a necessary and brave read."

—**PAUL KINGSNORTH**, novelist; founder, Dark Mountain Project

"There are moments in our history in which the art of the written word captures the extraordinary beauty of the human condition as it hangs suspended in tenuous polarity at a tipping point of evolution. *The Coronation* is one of these moments. In between these words that are as prophetic as they are poetic is the space of our collective metamorphosis. Tread lightly and dive deep here to find your own sovereign beauty." —**ZACH BUSH**, MD

"Charles Eisenstein is one of the most original writers working today, and his essays on the social and spiritual impact of the pandemic event are among his best work. *The Coronation* is essential reading for anyone concerned about the damage that has been done to our societies and how we might recover and collectively go forward from here."

—**C. J. HOPKINS**, award-winning playwright, novelist, and political satirist

The
Coronation

Also by Charles Eisenstein

The Ascent of Humanity
Sacred Economics
The More Beautiful World Our Hearts Know Is Possible
Climate: A New Story

The
Coronation

Essays from the Covid Moment

CHARLES EISENSTEIN

CHELSEA GREEN PUBLISHING
White River Junction, Vermont
London, UK

Project Manager: Patricia Stone
Project Editor: Brianne Goodspeed
Copy Editor: Diane Durrett
Proofreader: Tara Dugan
Designer: Melissa Jacobson

Printed in the United States of America.
First printing June 2022.
10 9 8 7 6 5 4 3 2 1   22 23 24 25 26

ISBN 978-1-64502-178-0 (paperback) | ISBN 978-1-64502-179-7 (ebook)
| ISBN 978-1-64502-180-3 (audio book)

Library of Congress Cataloging-in-Publication Data is available upon request.

Chelsea Green Publishing
85 North Main Street, Suite 120
White River Junction, Vermont USA

Somerset House
London, UK

www.chelseagreen.com

Dedicated to the children of our children.

Contents

Introduction

In India, I have heard, various faiths have made of Covid a new goddess, and installed her on their altars along with the rest. And why not? In pantheistic religions, the gods personify forces of man and nature, mediating the known and the unknowable. A goddess can be placated, propitiated, angered, or appeased, but never can she be conquered nor definitively understood.

The essays in this collection approach Covid from multiple directions. In part these reflect the evolution of my perspective over the last two years, but their multiplicity also bespeaks Covid's godlike ungraspability. What is Covid? In these pages I view it as a religious hysteria, as a disease pandemic, as a tool of totalitarian forces, and as an upheaval of latent Girardian sacrificial dynamics. Each of these lenses affords a view of features invisible from the others, yet none can fully capture the goddess Covid. That is why in many of the essays in this book I step back into a metaphysical vantage point, hesitating to reduce Covid to any one nameable thing.

The pattern of reductionism is in large part responsible for this horrifying mess we are in—the reduction of illness to pathogens, the reduction of public health to metrics, the reduction of citizens to medical objects. Let us not repeat the pattern by reducing the Covid phenomenon to one thing also. It is many things.

Whatever it is and is not, certainly Covid has wielded a mighty power, transforming society more than anything else in my lifetime. It has been apocalyptic, revealing in stark relief shadowy forces of the collective psyche. And of the individual psyche. And of my psyche! I know I am not alone in having undergone a deep journey in the time of Covid, even a kind of initiation. These essays trace that journey as each element of the collective psyche finds expression in me. The polar forces that Covid has flushed to the surface match similar hidden conflicts in myself, bubbling up for me to grapple with. These essays for the most part don't describe my inner process directly, but they certainly bear its trace. Defiance, despair, resignation, rage, doubt, hope, fear, dismay, conciliation, militancy—each takes its turn as author at some point in this book.

By the end, you will see where I have arrived as of the beginning of 2022. Covid has not finished with us yet. Even if it is declared over, it has set a process in motion that will play out over years and decades.

Among other things, Covid has revealed how close we are to totalitarianism. It took so little for its full machinery to spring into motion: surveillance, censorship, propaganda, restriction of movement, suspension of civil liberties. One explanation is that nefarious forces have been preparing for this moment for a long time. Perhaps. But to do so, they exploited psychosocial patterns and myths that are older than history. These will not easily disappear even if the pandemic is declared over and corrupt institutions and individuals punished. I explore these patterns and myths repeatedly throughout this book: the story of separation, the program of control, the myth of redemptive violence, the story of good versus evil, the paradigm of reductionism, the denial of death, the cult of quantity. As long as these patterns and myths remain intact, then even if the goddess Covid is exiled to the history books, they will soon draw in a successor.

As the threat of medical totalitarianism has not yet passed, I hesitate to retreat too far into the philosophical. It is time to speak out, directly, without hiding behind abstractions. But to ignore the conditions that have brought this civilizational illness upon us would be to commit the same error that motivates so much public health policy. If a virus of corruption, profit, and power has infected the body politic, let us not simply go to war against that virus without asking about the terrain.

Why are we so susceptible to hysteria? Why are we so susceptible to propaganda? Why are we so susceptible to fear? Why are we so susceptible to control-based solutioneering? What are the comorbidities that have made the body politic so weak? I have tried to illuminate these questions so that we might become more resistant to future infections of the totalitarian disease.

As these questions suggest, the source of our susceptibility lies deep in the collective psyche. To transform it requires nothing less than a total transformation of consciousness and culture, a profound shift in our basic mythology. Ultimately, as the Indian worshippers have recognized, Covid is a mythic event and must be addressed on that level. That is what I attempt to do in these essays—to render service to the goddess Covid in her quest to reveal what was hidden.

The illumination of that which was hidden can be a devastating event. Lies and delusions disintegrate, leaving the initiate bewildered, vulnerable, and afraid. Yet that moment also bears the possibility of liberation. It is an initiation from servitude into sovereignty. It is a coronation, when unconscious choices become conscious and hidden masters are exposed. Exposed, they lose their power, which all along depended on deception. The true master reclaims her crown.

That is the opportunity before us. It remains to be seen whether we will successfully pass the test. Will we claim true democracy? Will we reclaim life from the altar of safety? May this book be an ally to the part of you that says Yes.

Zika and the
Mentality of Control

This is the only essay in this collection that I wrote prior to the Covid era. The year was 2016. As this piece describes, all the ideological machinery was already in place for the transition that began in 2020 to a fully medicalized society.

Two years later, in 2018, I was given another preview of the age of lockdowns. My son Philip was to attend a school camp trip in Rhode Island. Unfortunately, two cases of Zika virus infection—a normally non-fatal mosquito-borne illness—had been discovered in New England, so the school authorities canceled the event in order to keep the children safe. To be outdoors, after all, means exposure to mosquitoes. Implicit in that decision is that the responsible thing to do as a parent would be to keep your child indoors at all times—something quite a few parents ended up doing. Yes, for weeks at a time, parents wouldn't let their children go outside. For me, the most crazy-making part of it was that no one seemed to think it was crazy.

This kind of decision raised a question that, though it is seldom stated explicitly in these terms, was to become an engine of social controversy in 2020: *How much of life shall we sacrifice at the altar of safety? If it keeps us a bit safer, should we never go outdoors again, never hug, never shake hands, never look upon each others' naked faces? Should we demand others do the same?*

As you read this essay, keep in mind that it was composed in 2016. The writing was already on the wall. The biosecurity state was just waiting for the right disease.

The ruling institutions of this world are quite comfortable with a virus.

First with SARS, then H1N1, then Ebola, and now the Zika virus, mainstream media and official organizations have been quick to recognize and counter the threat with travel advisories, quarantines, research funding, vaccine development, and heightened levels of vigilance. Yet information about other kinds of threats that are just as deadly, such as pharmaceutical residues in drinking water, pesticide contamination, or heavy metal poisoning from air and water pollution, are usually relegated to alternative media, ignored, or even actively suppressed by public health authorities. Why is this?

The ready answer that comes to mind is economic. The manmade threats listed above are by-products of profitable activities by corporations that have tremendous political influence. If we were to thoroughly address toxic contamination of our biosphere, our entire economic, industrial, medical, and agricultural system would have to change.

More deeply, a virus or other pathogen fits neatly into the basic crisis response template of our culture. First, identify an enemy—some unifactorial cause of the crisis—and then go to war against that enemy using all available technologies of control. In the case of a pathogen, control takes the form of antibiotics, vaccines, or antiviral agents, draining wetlands or spraying them with insecticides, quarantining infected individuals, and perhaps telling everyone to wear face masks, stay indoors, or restrict travel. In the case of terrorism, control takes the form of surveillance, bombings, drones, border security, and so on. Whatever crisis we face, personal or collective, our pseudo-instinctual tendency is to enact this pattern of response.

Another way to look at it is that in the case of an infectious disease, our society knows what to do (or thinks it knows what to do). The solutions that present themselves are comfortably familiar. We just have to do more of what we have already been doing. We just have to extend the reach of our control-based civilization a little further, control things that hadn't been under control before. Thus the machinery of containing or conquering a disease coincidentally aggrandizes agendas of social control generally. It justifies, exercises, and develops control systems that can be turned to other purposes.

The present situation with the Zika virus, which is blamed for a horrifying epidemic of microcephaly in Brazil, exemplifies a more general obsession with pathogens. Tests have shown the presence of the virus in the blood and amniotic fluid of some microcephalic fetuses in about one-tenth of confirmed cases in Brazil. However, Zika is also prevalent in Colombia and Venezuela, where no microcephaly outbreak has been reported.

The plot thickened a few weeks ago when a group of Argentinian doctors claimed that the outbreak is much more closely correlated with a larvicide aimed, ironically enough, at destroying the very mosquitoes that are blamed for the spread of Zika. The larvicide, called pyriproxyfen, was added to drinking water reservoirs in the same areas, and in the same time period, where microcephaly cases have surged.[1]

Obviously, it is much more politically convenient to blame an outside agent for the disease than for governments and large corporations to take responsibility. It is also more ideologically convenient from the perspective of the narrative of humanity ascending over nature. Rather than blame human activity, we can march against yet another threat from the natural world that we must overcome with a technological solution. That is something our culture is familiar with. Our institutions know how to do that; it exercises their capacities and justifies their existence.

Let us also be cautious, however, about identifying pyriproxyfen as "the cause" of the microcephaly. For one thing, the rush to blame a pesticide isn't that different from the rush to blame a virus. It still fits into the ideology of control and the mentality of defeating an enemy. In fact, some cases of microcephaly occurred in regions where the pesticide wasn't in the drinking water; pyriproxyfen, furthermore, is widely used around the world. It is a weak and circumstantial argument that identifies pyriproxyfen as the culprit.

In the preceding phrase (". . . the culprit") I have smuggled in an assumption that lies at the root of the problem. I am assuming there is "a" culprit, a unifactorial cause. Whether the culprit is a virus or a chemical, that gives us something to control, to fight. Whether it is over a virus or over a state government or chemical company, the path to victory is clear.

The ideology of control depends on reductionism, ideally reduction of a problem to a single cause. Multifactorial, nonlinear, emergent problems defy reductionistic strategies. So, while we should undoubtedly ban the use of pyriproxyfen in drinking water immediately, even if the microcephaly epidemic ceases, that doesn't mean we can continue business as normal and continue thinking in terms of linear cause and effect. Maybe it is Zika plus pyriproxyfen that is causing the deformities. Or maybe the chemical isn't a direct cause, but increases the effect of some third substance in the body. Or it could be that it disrupts the aquatic ecosystem in some way we don't understand that elevates another unknown environmental risk factor. We just don't know.

We need to ask questions like, "What are the ecosystem disruptions that occur when you kill larvae in *any* water (not just drinking water)?" "What are the cumulative and synergistic effects of thousands of artificial chemicals entering the biosphere and our bodies?" "How are we to make decisions about safety, when the usual means for testing safety is to control all variables except the one being tested?" You see, the paradigm of control extends all the way to a key formula for producing scientific knowledge: isolate a variable and test its effects.

Until we begin thinking in holistic terms, we will lurch from one enemy to the next, forever suppressing symptoms even as we worsen the disease. The questions above have no easy answers, but a good first step would be to pull back from the paradigm of dominating the enemy, controlling the Other, and conquering the self, and look with fresh eyes at everything we do from that paradigm: the drones, the prisons, the security state, the war machine, antibiotics, pesticides, genetic engineering, psychiatric medication, debt payment extraction . . . domination (including domination of "othered" parts of ourselves) threads through our entire civilization. It isn't working so well anymore.

The Coronation

I wrote "The Coronation" during the first month of the officially declared pandemic, when much about it was still in doubt. At that time, officials were warning of fatality rates of 4 percent and tens or hundreds of millions of deaths. Some of the essay's argumentation is no longer necessary, since now almost everyone accepts that fatality rates are at most a few tenths of a percent.

As is inevitable at such an early stage, there are some things I got wrong in this essay, and others that I offered as speculation and remain so today. For example, I underestimated the number of Americans who would die from the disease, although if those who died "with Covid" as opposed to "from Covid" are subtracted from the total, my numbers might not be so far off. Furthermore, many people died unnecessarily from inappropriate treatment with Remdesivir and ventilators, from the suppression of early treatment with natural, generic, and off-label medications, and from sending infected elderly people back to nursing homes.

Other things in the essay were prescient. First was my concern that the new health regime would be permanent (if we let it); that there will always be reason to stay locked down, masked, and distanced.

Remember, I wrote this when we were still being told the lockdowns were "two weeks to flatten the curve." There might be new viruses, I said. And so today we have an endless succession of variants. Those who thrive off control do not willingly relinquish it.

Whatever details I might have gotten right or wrong, in its broad strokes this essay is just as relevant now as it was two years ago. Maybe it is even more relevant. The myths and mindsets that allowed the virus of Covid hysteria to run rampant are still powerful, and now as the fiasco of the pandemic response becomes plain, we have a unique opportunity for collective soul-searching. That is why I am putting so much energy into recirculating these essays, particularly "The Coronation."

"The Coronation" provoked controversy and condemnation. This response gave me insight into the information war that soon became woven into the war on Covid, in which any criticism of the orthodox narrative is branded as conspiracy theorizing, Trumpism, or some kind of psychopathology.

Even though it was ultimately read by over two million people (on my website alone), the core themes of the essay were ignored by critics. To this day, issues of death phobia, health-as-relationship, and the paradigm of control get lost in endless debating about studies and statistics about vaccines, masks, and so forth. The real issue, the defining choice at the crossroads this essay describes, remains: What kind of world shall we live in?

F or years, normality has been stretched nearly to its breaking point, a rope pulled tighter and tighter, waiting for a nip of the black swan's beak to snap it in two. Now that the rope has snapped, do we tie its ends back together, or shall we undo its dangling braids still further, to see what we might weave from them?

Covid-19 is showing us that when humanity is united in common cause, phenomenally rapid change is possible. None of the world's problems are technically difficult to solve; they originate in human disagreement. In coherency, humanity's creative powers are boundless. A few months ago, a proposal to halt commercial air travel would have seemed preposterous. Likewise for the radical changes we are making in our social behavior, economy, and the role of government in our lives. Covid demonstrates the power of our collective will when we agree on what is important. What else might we achieve, in coherency? What do we want to achieve, and what world shall we create? That is always the next question when anyone awakens to their power.

Covid-19 is like a rehab intervention that breaks the addictive hold of normality. To interrupt a habit is to make it visible; it is to turn it from a compulsion to a choice. When the crisis subsides, we might have occasion to ask whether we want to return to normal, or whether there might be something we've seen during this break in the routines that we want to bring into the future. We might ask, after so many have lost their jobs, whether these are the jobs the world most needs, and whether our labor and creativity would be better applied elsewhere. We might ask, having done without it for a while, whether we really need so much air travel, Disney World vacations, or trade shows. What parts of the economy will we want to restore, and what parts might we choose to let go of? Covid has interrupted what looked to be a military regime-change operation in Venezuela—perhaps imperialist wars are also one of those things we might relinquish in a future of global cooperation. And on a darker note, what among the things that are being taken away right now—civil liberties, freedom of assembly, sovereignty over our bodies, in-person gatherings, hugs, handshakes, and public life—might we need to exert intentional political and personal will to restore?

For most of my life, I have had the feeling that humanity was nearing a crossroads. Always, the crisis, the collapse, the break was imminent, just around the bend, but it didn't come and it didn't come. Imagine walking a road, and up ahead you see it, you see the crossroads. It's just over the hill, around the bend, past the woods. Cresting the hill, you see you were mistaken; it was a mirage; it was farther away than you thought. You keep walking. Sometimes it comes into view, sometimes it disappears from sight and it seems like this road goes on forever. Maybe there isn't a crossroads. No, there it is again! Always it is almost here. Never is it here.

Now, all of a sudden, we go around a bend and here it is. We stop, hardly able to believe that now it is happening, hardly able to believe, after years of confinement to the road of our predecessors, that now we finally have a choice. We are right to stop, stunned at the newness of our situation. Of the hundred paths that radiate out in front of us, some lead in the same direction we've already been headed. Some lead to hell on earth. And some lead to a world more healed and more beautiful than we ever dared believe to be possible.

I write these words with the aim of standing here with you—bewildered, scared maybe, yet also with a sense of new possibility—at this point of diverging paths. Let us gaze down some of them and see where they lead.

———

I heard this story last week from a friend. She was in a grocery store and saw a woman sobbing in the aisle. Flouting social distancing rules, she went to the woman and gave her a hug. "Thank you," the woman said, "that is the first time anyone has hugged me for ten days."

Going without hugs for a few weeks seems a small price to pay if it will stem an epidemic that could take millions of lives. Initially, the argument for social distancing was that it would save millions by preventing a sudden surge of Covid cases from overwhelming the medical system. Now the authorities tell us that some social distancing may need to continue indefinitely, at least until there is an effective vaccine. I would like to put that argument in a larger context, especially as we look to the long term. Lest we institutionalize distancing and reengineer society around it, let us be aware of what choice we are making and why.

The same goes for the other changes happening around the coronavirus epidemic. Some commentators have observed how it plays neatly into an agenda of totalitarian control. A frightened public accepts abridgments of civil liberties that are otherwise hard to justify, such as the tracking of everyone's movements at all times, forcible medical treatment, involuntary quarantine, restrictions on travel and the freedom of assembly, censorship of what the authorities deem to be disinformation, suspension of habeas corpus, and military policing of civilians. Many of these were underway before Covid-19; since its advent, they have been unstoppable. The same goes for the automation of commerce; the transition from participation in sports and entertainment to remote viewing; the migration of life from public to private spaces; the transition away from place-based schools toward online education; the destruction of small business; the decline of brick-and-mortar stores; and the movement of human work and leisure onto screens. Covid-19 is accelerating preexisting trends, political, economic, and social.

While all such abridgments and transitions are, in the short term, justified on the grounds of flattening the curve (the epidemiological growth curve), we are also hearing a lot about a "new normal"; that is to say, the changes may not be temporary at all. Since the threat of infectious disease, like the threat of terrorism, never goes away, control measures can easily become permanent. If we were going in this direction anyway, the current justification must be part of a deeper impulse. I will analyze this impulse in terms of a cultural reflex of control and its associated war on death. Thus understood, an initiatory opportunity emerges, one that we are seeing already in the form of the solidarity, compassion, and care that Covid-19 has inspired.

The Reflex of Control

Nearing the end of April 2020, official statistics say that about 150,000 people have died from Covid-19. By the time it runs its course, the death toll could be ten times or a hundred times bigger. Each one of these people has loved ones, family, and friends. Compassion and conscience call us to do what we can to avert unnecessary tragedy. This is personal for me: My own infinitely dear but frail mother is among the most vulnerable to a disease that kills mostly the aged and the infirm.

What will the final numbers be? That question is impossible to answer at the time of this writing. Early reports were alarming; for weeks the official number from Wuhan, China, circulated endlessly in the media, was a shocking 3.4 percent. That, coupled with its highly contagious nature, pointed to tens of millions of deaths worldwide, or even as many as 100 million. More recently, estimates have plunged as it has become apparent that most cases are mild or asymptomatic. Since testing has been skewed toward the seriously ill, the death rate has looked artificially high. A recent paper in the journal *Science* argues that 86 percent of infections have been undocumented, which points to a much lower mortality rate than the current case fatality rate would indicate.[1] Another goes even further, estimating total US infections at a hundred times current confirmed cases (which would mean a case fatality rate [CFR] of less than 0.1 percent).[2] These papers involve a lot of fancy epidemiological guesswork, but a very recent study using an antibody test found that cases in Santa Clara, California have been vastly underreported.[3]

The story of the *Diamond Princess* cruise ship bolsters this view. Of the 3,711 people on board, about 20 percent tested positive for the virus; less than half of those had symptoms, and 8 died. A cruise ship is a perfect setting for contagion, and there was plenty of time for the virus to spread on board before anyone did anything about it, yet only a fifth were infected. Furthermore, the cruise ship's population was heavily skewed (as are most cruise ships) toward the elderly: Nearly a third of the passengers were over age seventy, and more than half were over age sixty. A research team concluded from the large number of asymptomatic cases that the true fatality rate in China is around 0.5 percent; more recent data indicates a figure closer to 0.2 percent.[4] That is still two to five times higher than seasonal flu. Based on these findings (and adjusting for much younger demographics in Africa, South Asia, and Southeast Asia) my guess is that Covid-19 will cause about 200,000–300,000 deaths in the US and two million globally. Those are serious numbers, comparable to the Hong Kong Flu pandemic of 1968–9.

Every day the media reports the total number of Covid-19 cases, but no one has any idea what the true number is, because only a tiny proportion of the population has been tested. If tens of millions have the virus, asymptomatically, we would not know it. Further complicating the matter is that Covid-19 deaths may be overreported (in many hospitals, if someone dies *with* Covid they are recorded as having died *from* Covid) or underreported (some may have died at home). Let me repeat: No one knows what is really happening, including me. Let us be aware of two contradictory tendencies in human affairs. The first is the tendency for hysteria to feed on itself, to exclude data points that don't play into the fear, and to create the world in its image. The second is denial, the irrational rejection of information that might disrupt normalcy and comfort.

Cognitive biases such as these are especially virulent in an atmosphere of political polarization; for example, liberals will tend to reject any information that might be woven into a pro-Trump narrative, while conservatives will tend to embrace it.

In the face of the uncertainty, I'd like to make a prediction: The crisis will play out so that we never will know. If the final death tally, which will itself be the subject of dispute, is lower than feared, some will say that is because the controls worked. Others will say it is because the disease wasn't as dangerous as we were told.

To me, the most baffling puzzle is why at the present writing there seem to be no new cases in China. The government didn't initiate its lockdown until well after the virus was established. It should have spread widely during Chinese New Year, when, despite a few travel restrictions, nearly every plane, train, and bus was packed with people traveling all over the country. What is going on here? Again, I don't know, and neither do you.

Whatever the final death toll, let's look at some other numbers to get some perspective. My point is *not* that Covid isn't so bad and we shouldn't do anything. Bear with me. As of 2013, according to the Food and Agriculture Organization (FAO), 5 million children worldwide die every year of hunger; in 2018, 159 million children were stunted and 50 million were wasted.[5] (Hunger was falling until recently, but has started to rise again in the last three years.) Five million is many times more people than have died so far from Covid-19, yet no government has declared a state of emergency or asked that we radically alter our way of life to save them. Nor do we see a comparable level of alarm and action around suicide—the mere tip of an iceberg of despair and depression—which kills over a million people a year globally and 50,000 in the US. Or drug overdoses, which kill 70,000 in the US; or the autoimmunity epidemic, which affects anywhere from 23.5 million according to figures from the National Institutes of Health (NIH) to 50 million according to American Autoimmune Related Diseases Association (AARDA); or obesity, which afflicts well over 100 million. Why, for that matter, are we not in a frenzy about averting nuclear

Armageddon or ecological collapse, but, to the contrary, pursue choices that magnify those very dangers?

Please, the point here is not that we haven't changed our ways to stop children from starving, so we shouldn't change them for Covid, either. It is the contrary: If we can change so radically for Covid-19, we can do it for these other conditions, too. Let us ask why are we able to unify our collective will to stem this virus, but not to address other grave threats to humanity. Why, until now, has society been so frozen in its existing trajectory?

The answer is revealing. Simply, in the face of world hunger, addiction, autoimmunity, suicide, or ecological collapse, we as a society do not know what to do. That's because there is nothing external against which to fight. Our go-to crisis responses, all of which are some version of control, aren't very effective in addressing these conditions. Now along comes a contagious epidemic, and finally we can spring into action. It is a crisis for which control works: quarantines, lockdowns, isolation, handwashing; control of movement, control of information, control of our bodies. That makes Covid a convenient receptacle for our inchoate fears, a place to channel our growing sense of helplessness in the face of the changes overtaking the world. Covid-19 is a threat that we know how to meet. Unlike so many of our other fears, Covid-19 offers a plan.

Our civilization's established institutions are increasingly helpless to meet the challenges of our time. How they welcome a challenge that they finally can meet. How eager they are to embrace it as a paramount crisis. How naturally their systems of information management select for the most alarming portrayals of it. How easily the public joins the panic, embracing a threat that the authorities can handle as a proxy for the various unspeakable threats that they cannot.

Today, most of our challenges no longer succumb to force. Our antibiotics and surgery fail to meet the surging health crises of autoimmunity, addiction, and obesity. Our guns and bombs, built to conquer armies, are useless to erase hatred abroad or keep domestic violence out of our homes. Our police and prisons cannot heal the breeding conditions of crime. Our pesticides cannot restore ruined soil. Covid-19 recalls the good old days when the challenges of infectious diseases succumbed to modern medicine and hygiene, at the same time as the Nazis succumbed to the war machine, and nature itself succumbed, or so it seemed, to technological conquest and improvement. It recalls the days when our weapons worked and the world seemed indeed to be improving with each technology of control.

What kind of problem succumbs to domination and control? The kind caused by something from the outside, something Other. When the cause of the problem is something intimate to ourselves, like homelessness or inequality, addiction or obesity, there is nothing to war against. We may try to install an enemy, blaming, for example, the billionaires, Vladimir Putin, or the Devil, but then we miss key information, such as the ground conditions that allow billionaires (or viruses) to replicate in the first place.

If there is one thing our civilization is good at, it is fighting an enemy. We welcome opportunities to do what we are good at, which prove the validity of our technologies, systems, and worldview. And so we manufacture enemies, cast problems like crime, terrorism, and disease into us-versus-them terms, and mobilize our collective energies toward those endeavors that can be seen that way. Thus, we single out Covid-19 as a call to arms, reorganizing society as if for a war effort, while treating as normal the possibility of nuclear Armageddon, ecological collapse, and five million children starving.

The Conspiracy Narrative
Because Covid-19 seems to justify so many items on the totalitarian wish list, there are those who believe it to be a deliberate

power play. It is not my purpose to advance that theory nor to debunk it, although I will offer some meta-level comments. First a brief overview.

The theories (there are many variants) talk about a simulation exercise known as Event 201 (sponsored by the Bill and Melinda Gates Foundation, the CIA, and others in October 2019), and a 2010 white paper by The Rockefeller Foundation detailing a scenario called Lockstep. Both of these scenarios lay out the authoritarian response to a hypothetical pandemic. They observe that the infrastructure, technology, and legislative framework for martial law has been in preparation for many years. All that was needed, they say, was a way to make the public embrace it, and now that has come. Whether or not current controls are permanent, a precedent is being set for:

- The tracking of people's movements at all times (because coronavirus)
- The suspension of freedom of assembly (because coronavirus)
- The military policing of civilians (because coronavirus)
- Extrajudicial, indefinite detention (quarantine, because coronavirus)
- The banning of cash (because coronavirus)
- Censorship of the internet (to combat disinformation, because coronavirus)
- Compulsory vaccination and other medical treatment, establishing the state's sovereignty over our bodies (because coronavirus)
- The classification of all activities and destinations into the expressly permitted and the expressly forbidden (you can leave your house for this, but not that), eliminating the unpoliced, nonjuridical gray zone. That totality is the very essence of totalitarianism. Necessary now though, because, well, coronavirus.

This is juicy material for conspiracy theories. For all I know, one of those theories could be true; however, the same progression of events could unfold from an unconscious systemic tilt toward ever-increasing control. Where does this tilt come from? It is woven into civilization's DNA. For millennia, civilization (as opposed to small-scale traditional cultures) has understood progress as a matter of extending control onto the world: domesticating the wild, conquering the barbarians, mastering the forces of nature, and ordering society according to law and reason. The ascent of control accelerated with the Scientific Revolution, which launched "progress" to new heights: the ordering of reality into objective categories and quantities, and the mastering of materiality with technology. Finally, the social sciences promised to use the same means and methods to fulfill the ambition (which goes back to Plato and Confucius) to engineer a perfect society.

Those who administer civilization will therefore welcome any opportunity to strengthen their control, for after all, it is in service to a grand vision of human destiny: the perfectly ordered world, in which disease, crime, poverty, and perhaps suffering itself can be engineered out of existence. No nefarious motives are necessary. Of course they would like to keep track of everyone—all the better to ensure the common good. For them, Covid-19 shows how necessary that is. "Can we afford democratic freedoms in light of the coronavirus?" they ask. "Must we now, out of necessity, sacrifice those for our own safety?" It is a familiar refrain, for it has accompanied other crises in the past, like 9/11.

To rework a common metaphor, imagine a man with a hammer, stalking around looking for a reason to use it. Suddenly he sees a nail sticking out. He's been looking for a nail for a long time, pounding on screws and bolts and not accomplishing much. He inhabits a worldview in which hammers are the best tools, and the world can be made better by pounding in the nails.

And here is a nail! We might suspect that in his eagerness he has placed the nail there himself, but it hardly matters. Maybe it isn't even a nail that's sticking out, but it resembles one enough to start pounding. When the tool is at the ready, an opportunity will arise to use it.

And I will add, for those inclined to doubt the authorities, maybe this time it really is a nail. In that case, the hammer is the right tool—and the hammer will emerge all the stronger, ready now to conquer the screw, the button, the clip, and the tear.

Either way, the problem we deal with here is much deeper than that of overthrowing an evil coterie of Illuminati. Even if they do exist, given the tilt of civilization, the same trend would persist without them, or a new Illuminati would arise to assume the functions of the old.

True or false, the idea that the epidemic is some monstrous plot perpetrated by evildoers upon the public is not so far from the mindset of find-the-pathogen. It is a crusading mentality, a war mentality. It locates the source of a sociopolitical illness in a pathogen against which we may then fight, a victimizer separate from ourselves. It risks ignoring the conditions that make society fertile ground for the plot to take hold. Whether that ground was sown deliberately or by the wind is a secondary question.

What I will say next about our society's relationship to death is relevant whether or not SARS-CoV-2 is a genetically engineered bioweapon, is related to the 5G rollout, is being used to prevent "disclosure," is a Trojan horse for totalitarian world government, is more deadly than we've been told, is less deadly than we've been told, originated in a Wuhan biolab, originated at Fort Detrick, or is exactly as the Centers for Disease Control and Prevention (CDC) and World Health Organization (WHO) have been telling us. It applies even if everyone is totally wrong about the role of the SARS-CoV-2 virus in the current epidemic. I have my opinions, but if there is one thing I have learned through the course of this emergency is that I don't really know what is happening. I don't see how anyone can, amidst the seething farrago of news, fake news, rumors, suppressed information, conspiracy theories, propaganda, and politicized narratives that fill the internet. I wish a lot more people would embrace not knowing. I say that both to those who embrace the dominant narrative, as well as to those who hew to dissenting ones. What information might we be blocking out, in order to maintain the integrity of our viewpoints? Let's be humble in our beliefs: It is a matter of life and death.

The War on Death

My seven-year-old son hasn't seen or played with another child for two weeks. Millions of others are in the same boat. Most would agree that a month without social interaction for all those children is a reasonable sacrifice to save a million lives. But how about to save 100,000 lives? And what if the sacrifice is not for a month but for a year? Five years? Different people will have different opinions on that, according to their underlying values.

Let's replace the foregoing questions with something more personal, something that pierces the inhuman utilitarian thinking that turns people into statistics and sacrifices some of them for something else. A relevant question for me is, Would I ask all the nation's children to forego play for a season, if it would reduce my mother's risk of dying, or for that matter, my own risk? Or I might ask, Would I decree the end of human hugging and handshakes, if it would save my own life? This is not to devalue Mom's life or my own, both of which are precious. I am grateful for every day she is still with us. But these questions bring up deep issues. What is the right way to live? What is the right way to die?

The answer to such questions, whether asked on behalf of oneself or on behalf of society at large, depends on how we relate to death and how much we value play, touch, and togetherness, along with civil liberties and personal freedom, in comparison to safety. There is no easy formula to balance these values.

Over my lifetime I've seen society place more and more emphasis on safety, security, and risk reduction. It has especially impacted childhood: When I was a young boy it was normal for us to roam a mile from home unsupervised—behavior that would earn parents a visit from Child Protective Services today. It also manifests in the form of latex gloves for more and more professions; hand sanitizer everywhere; locked, guarded, and surveilled school buildings; intensified airport and border security; heightened awareness of legal liability and liability insurance; metal detectors and searches before entering many sports arenas and public buildings, and so on. Writ large, it takes the form of the security state.

The mantra "safety first" comes from a value system that makes survival top priority, and that depreciates other values like fun, adventure, play, and the challenging of limits. Other cultures have different priorities. For instance, many traditional and indigenous cultures are much less protective of children, as documented in Jean Liedloff's classic, *The Continuum Concept*. These societies allow children to take risks and have responsibilities that would seem insane to most modern people, believing that this is necessary for children to develop self-reliance and good judgment. I think most modern people, especially younger people, retain some of this inherent willingness to sacrifice safety in order to live life fully. The surrounding culture, however, lobbies us relentlessly to live in fear, and has constructed systems that embody fear. In them, staying safe is overridingly important. Thus we have a medical system in which most decisions are based on calculations of risk, and in which the worst possible outcome, marking the physician's ultimate failure, is death. Yet all the while, we know that death awaits us regardless. A life saved actually means a death postponed.

The ultimate fulfillment of civilization's program of control would be to triumph over death itself. Failing that, modern society settles for a facsimile of that triumph: denial rather than conquest. Ours is a society of death denial, from its hiding away of corpses, to its fetish for youthfulness, to its warehousing of old people in nursing homes. Even its obsession with money and property—extensions of the self, as the word "mine" indicates in association with ownership—expresses the delusion that the impermanent self can be made permanent through its attachments. All this is inevitable given the story-of-self that modernity offers: the separate individual in a world of Other. Surrounded by genetic, social, and economic competitors, that self must protect and dominate in order to thrive. It must do everything it can to forestall death, which (in the story of separation) is total annihilation. Biological science has even taught us that our very nature is to maximize our chances of surviving and reproducing.

I asked a friend, a medical doctor who has spent time with the Q'ero in Peru, whether the Q'ero would (if they could) intubate someone to prolong their life. "Of course not," she said. "They would summon the shaman to help him die well." Dying well (which isn't necessarily the same as dying painlessly) is not much in today's medical vocabulary. No hospital records are kept on whether patients die well. That would not be counted as a positive outcome. In the world of the separate self, death is the ultimate catastrophe.

But is it? Consider this perspective from Dr. Lissa Rankin: "Not all of us would want to be in an ICU, isolated from loved ones with a machine breathing for us, at risk of dying alone—even if it means they might increase their chance of survival. Some of us might rather be held in the arms of loved ones at home, even if that means our time has come. . . . Remember, death is no ending. Death is going home."[6]

When the self is understood as relational, interdependent, even inter-existent, then it bleeds over into the other, and the other bleeds over into the self. Understanding the self as a locus of consciousness in a matrix of relationships, one no longer searches for an enemy as the key to understanding every problem, but looks instead for imbalances in relationships. The war on death gives way to the quest to live well and fully, and we see that fear of death is actually fear of life. How much of life will we forego to stay safe?

Totalitarianism—the perfection of control—is the inevitable end product of the mythology of the separate self. What else but a threat to life, like a war, would merit total control? Thus Orwell identified perpetual war as a crucial component of the Party's rule.

Against the backdrop of the program of control, death denial, and the separate self, the assumption that public policy should seek to minimize the number of deaths is nearly beyond question, a goal to which other values like play, freedom, and so forth are subordinate. Covid-19 offers occasion to broaden that view. Yes, let us hold life sacred, more sacred than ever. Death teaches us that. Let us hold each person, young or old, sick or well, as the sacred, precious, beloved being that they are. And in the circle of our hearts, let us make room for other sacred values, too. To hold life sacred is not just to live long, it is to live well and right and fully.

Like all fear, the fear around the coronavirus hints at what might lie beyond it. Anyone who has experienced the passing of someone close knows that death is a portal to love. Covid-19 has elevated death to prominence in the consciousness of a society that denies it. On the other side of the fear, we can see the love that death liberates. Let it pour forth. Let it saturate the soil of our culture and fill its aquifers so that it seeps up through the cracks of our crusted institutions, our systems, and our habits. Some of these may die, too.

What World Shall We Live In?

How much of life do we want to sacrifice at the altar of security? If it keeps us safer, do we want to live in a world where human beings never congregate? Do we want to wear masks in public all the time? Do we want to be medically examined every time we travel, if that will save some number of lives a year? Are we willing to accept the medicalization of life in general, handing over final sovereignty over our bodies to medical authorities (as selected by political ones)? Do we want every event to be a virtual event? How much are we willing to live in fear?

Covid-19 will eventually subside, but the threat of infectious disease is permanent. Our response to it sets a course for the future. Public life, communal life, the life of shared physicality has been dwindling over several generations. Instead of shopping at stores, we get things delivered to our homes. Instead of packs of kids playing outside, we have playdates and digital adventures. Instead of the public square, we have the online forum. Do we want to continue to insulate ourselves still further from each other and the world?

It is not hard to imagine, especially if social distancing is successful, that Covid-19 persists beyond the eighteen months we are being told to expect for it to run its course. It is not hard to imagine that new viruses will emerge during that time. It is not hard to imagine that emergency measures will become normal (so as to forestall the possibility of another outbreak), just as the state of emergency declared after 9/11 is still in effect today. It is not hard to imagine that (as we are being told), rein-fection is possible, so that the disease will never run its course. That means that the temporary changes in our way of life may become permanent.

To reduce the risk of another pandemic, shall we choose to live in a society without hugs, handshakes, and high-fives, forever more? Shall we choose to live in a society where we no longer gather en masse? Shall the concert, the sports competition, and the festival be a thing of the past? Shall children no longer play with other children? Shall all human contact be mediated by computers and masks? No more dance classes, no more karate classes, no more conferences, no more churches? Is death reduction to be the standard by which to measure progress? Does human advancement mean separation? Is this the future?

The same question applies to the administrative tools required to control the movement of people and the flow of information. At the present writing, the entire country is moving toward lockdown. In some countries, one must print out a form from a government website in order to leave the house. It reminds me of school, where one's location must be authorized at all times. Or of prison. Do we envision a future of electronic hall passes, a system where freedom of movement is governed by state administrators and their software at all times, permanently? Where every movement is tracked, either permitted or prohibited? And, for our protection, where information that threatens our health (as decided, again, by various authorities) is censored for our own good? In the face of an emergency, like unto a state of war, we accept such restrictions and temporarily surrender our freedoms. Similar to 9/11, Covid-19 trumps all objections.

For the first time in history, the technological means exist to realize such a vision, at least in the developed world (for example, using cell phone location data to enforce social distancing). After a bumpy transition, we could live in a society where nearly all of life happens online: shopping, meeting, entertainment, socializing, working, even dating. Is that what we want? How many lives saved is that worth?

I am sure that many of the controls in effect today will be partially relaxed in a few months. Partially relaxed, but at the ready. As long as infectious disease remains with us, they are likely to be reimposed, again and again, in the future, or be self-imposed in the form of habits. As Deborah Tannen says, contributing to a *Politico* article on how coronavirus will change the world permanently, "We know now that touching things, being with other people and breathing the air in an enclosed space can be risky. . . . It could become second nature to recoil from shaking hands or touching our faces—and we may all fall heir to society-wide OCD, as none of us can stop washing our hands."[7] After thousands of years, millions of years, of touch, contact, and togetherness, is the pinnacle of human progress to be that we cease such activities because they are too risky?

Life Is Community

The paradox of the program of control is that its progress rarely advances us any closer to its goal. Despite security systems in almost every upper middle-class home, people are no less anxious or insecure than they were a generation ago. Despite elaborate security measures, the schools are not seeing fewer mass shootings. Despite phenomenal progress in medical technology, people have if anything become less healthy over the past thirty years, as chronic disease has proliferated and life expectancy stagnated and, in the US and Britain, started to decline.

The measures being instituted to control Covid-19, likewise, may end up causing more suffering and death than they prevent. Minimizing deaths means minimizing the deaths that we know how to predict and measure. It is impossible to measure the added deaths that might come from isolation-induced depression, for instance, or the despair caused by unemployment, or the lowered immunity and deterioration in health that chronic fear can cause.[8] Loneliness and lack of social contact has been shown to increase inflammation, depression, and dementia.[9] According to Dr. Lissa Rankin, air pollution increases the risk of dying by 6 percent, obesity by 23 percent, alcohol abuse by 37 percent, and loneliness by 45 percent.[10]

Another danger that is off the ledger is the deterioration in immunity caused by excessive hygiene and distancing. It is not only social contact that is necessary for health, it is also contact with the microbial world. Generally speaking, microbes are not our enemies, but are our allies in health. A diverse gut biome, comprising bacteria, viruses, yeasts, and other organisms, is essential for a well-functioning immune system, and its diversity is maintained through contact with other people and with the world of life. Excessive handwashing, overuse of antibiotics, aseptic cleanliness, and lack of human contact might do more harm than good.[11] The resulting allergies and autoimmune disorders might be worse than the infectious disease they replace. Socially and biologically, health comes from community. Life does not thrive in isolation.

Seeing the world in us-versus-them terms blinds us to the reality that life and health happen in community. To take the example of infectious diseases, we fail to look beyond the evil pathogen and ask, What is the role of viruses in the microbiome?[12] What are the body conditions under which harmful viruses proliferate? Why do some people have mild symptoms and others severe ones (besides the catch-all nonexplanation of "low resistance")? What positive role might flus, colds, and other nonlethal diseases play in the maintenance of health?

War-on-germs thinking brings results akin to those of the War on Terror, War on Crime, War on Weeds, and the endless wars we fight politically and interpersonally. First, it generates endless war; second, it diverts attention from the ground conditions that breed illness, terrorism, crime, weeds, and the rest.

Despite politicians' perennial claim that they pursue war for the sake of peace, war inevitably breeds more war. Bombing countries to kill terrorists not only ignores the ground conditions of terrorism, it exacerbates those conditions. Locking up criminals not only ignores the conditions that breed crime, it creates those conditions when it breaks up families and communities and acculturates the incarcerated to criminality. And regimes of antibiotics, vaccines, antivirals, and other medicines wreak havoc on body ecology, which is the foundation of strong immunity. Outside the body, the massive spraying campaigns sparked by

Zika, dengue fever, and now Covid-19 will visit untold damage upon nature's ecology. Has anyone considered what the effects on the ecosystem will be when we douse it with antiviral compounds? Such a policy (which has been implemented in various places in China and India) is only thinkable from the mindset of separation, which does not understand that viruses are integral to the web of life.

To understand the point about ground conditions, consider some mortality statistics from Italy (from its National Institute of Health), based on an analysis of hundreds of Covid-19 fatalities.[13] Of those analyzed, less than 1 percent were free of serious chronic health conditions. Some 75 percent suffered from hypertension, 35 percent from diabetes, 33 percent from cardiac ischemia, 24 percent from atrial fibrillation, 18 percent from low renal function, along with other conditions. Nearly half the deceased had three or more of these serious pathologies. Americans, beset by obesity, diabetes, and other chronic ailments, are at least as vulnerable as Italians. Should we blame the virus then (which killed few otherwise healthy people), or shall we blame underlying poor health? Here again the analogy of the taut rope applies. Millions of people in the modern world are in a precarious state of health, just waiting for something that would normally be trivial to send them over the edge. Of course, in the short term we want to save their lives; the danger is that we lose ourselves in an endless succession of short terms, fighting one infectious disease after another, and never engage the ground conditions that make people so vulnerable. That is a much harder problem, because these ground conditions will not change via fighting. There is no pathogen that causes diabetes or obesity, addiction, depression, or PTSD. Their causes are not an Other, not some virus separate from ourselves, and we its victims.

Even in diseases like Covid-19, in which we can name a pathogenic virus, matters are not so simple as a war between virus and victim. There is an alternative to the germ theory of disease that holds germs to be part of a larger process. When conditions are right, they multiply in the body, sometimes killing the host, but also, potentially, improving the conditions that accommodated them to begin with, for example by cleaning out accumulated toxic debris via mucus discharge, or (metaphorically speaking) burning them up with fever. This "terrain theory," as it is sometimes called, says that germs are more symptom than cause of disease. As one meme explains it: "Your fish is sick. Germ theory: isolate the fish. Terrain theory: clean the tank."

A certain schizophrenia afflicts the modern culture of health. On the one hand, there is a burgeoning wellness movement that embraces alternative and holistic medicine. It advocates herbs, meditation, and yoga to boost immunity. It validates the emotional and spiritual dimensions of health, such as the power of attitudes and beliefs to sicken or to heal. All of this seems to have disappeared under the Covid tsunami, as society defaults to the old orthodoxy.

Case in point: California acupuncturists have been forced to shut down, having been deemed "nonessential." This is perfectly understandable from the perspective of conventional virology. But as one acupuncturist on Facebook observed, "What about my patient who I'm working with to get off opioids for his back pain? He's going to have to start using them again." From the worldview of medical authority, alternative modalities, social interaction, yoga classes, supplements, and so on are frivolous when it comes to real diseases caused by real viruses. They are relegated to an etheric realm of "wellness" in the face of a crisis. The resurgence of orthodoxy under Covid-19 is so intense that anything remotely unconventional, such as intravenous vitamin C, was completely off the table in the United States until two days ago (articles still abound "debunking" the "myth" that vitamin C can help fight Covid-19). Nor have I heard the CDC evangelize the benefits of elderberry extract, medicinal mushrooms, cutting sugar intake, NAC (N-acetyl L-cysteine), astragalus, or vitamin D. These are not just mushy speculations about "wellness," but are supported by extensive research and physiological explanations. For example, NAC has been shown to radically reduce incidence and severity of symptoms in flu-like illnesses.[14]

As the statistics I offered earlier on autoimmunity, obesity, and the like indicate, America and the modern world in general are facing a health crisis. Is the answer to do what we've been doing, only more thoroughly? The response so far to Covid has been to double down on the orthodoxy and sweep unconventional practices and dissenting viewpoints aside. Another response would be to widen our lens and examine the entire system, including who pays for it, how access is granted, and how research is funded; and also expand out to examine marginal fields like herbal medicine, functional medicine, and energy medicine. Perhaps we can take this opportunity to reevaluate prevailing theories of illness, health, and the body. Yes, let's protect the sickened fish as best we can right now, but maybe next time we won't have to isolate and drug so many fish, if we can clean the tank.

I'm not telling you to run out right now and buy NAC or any other supplement, nor that we as a society should abruptly shift our response, cease social distancing immediately, and start taking supplements instead. But we can use this break in normality, this pause at a crossroads, to consciously choose what path we shall follow moving forward: what kind of health care system, what paradigm of health, what kind of society. This reevaluation is already happening, as ideas like universal free health care in the US gain new momentum. And that path leads to forks, as well. What kind of health care will be universalized? Will it be merely available to all, or mandatory for all—each citizen a patient, perhaps with an invisible ink barcode tattoo certifying one is up to date on all compulsory vaccines and checkups? Then you can go to school, board a plane, or enter a restaurant. This is one path to the future that is available to us.

Another option is available now, too. Instead of doubling down on control, we could finally embrace the holistic paradigms and practices that have been waiting on the margins, waiting for the center to dissolve so that, in our humbled state, we can bring them into the center and build a new system around them.

The Coronation

There is an alternative to the paradise of perfect control that our civilization has so long pursued, and that recedes as fast as our progress, like a mirage on the horizon. Yes, we can proceed as before down the path toward greater insulation, isolation, domination, and separation. We can normalize heightened levels of separation and control, believe that they are necessary to keep us safe, and accept a world in which we are afraid to be near each other. Or we can take advantage of this pause, this break in normality, to turn onto a path of reunion, of holism, of the restoring of lost connections, of the repair of community and the rejoining of the web of life.

Do we double down on protecting the separate self, or do we accept the invitation into a world where all of us are in this together? It isn't just in medicine we encounter this question: it visits us politically, economically, and in our personal lives, as well. Take for example the issue of hoarding, which embodies the idea, "There won't be enough for everyone, so I am going to make sure there is enough for me." Another response might be, "Some don't have enough, so I will share what I have with them." Are we to be survivalists or helpers? What is life for?

On a larger scale, people are asking questions that have until now lurked on activist margins. What should we do about the homeless? What should we do about the people in prisons? In Third World slums? What should we do about the unemployed?

What about all the hotel maids, the Uber drivers, the plumbers and janitors and bus drivers and cashiers who cannot work from home? And so now, finally, ideas like student debt relief and universal basic income are blossoming. "How do we protect those susceptible to Covid?" invites us into "How do we care for vulnerable people in general?"

That is the impulse that stirs in us, regardless of the superficialities of our opinions about Covid's severity, origin, or best policy to address it. It is saying, let's get serious about taking care of each other. Let's remember how precious we all are and how precious life is. Let's take inventory of our civilization, strip it down to its studs, and see if we can build one more beautiful.

As Covid stirs our compassion, more and more of us realize that we don't want to go back to a normal so sorely lacking it. We have the opportunity now to forge a new, more compassionate normal.

Hopeful signs abound that this is happening. The United States government, which has long seemed the captive of heartless corporate interests, has unleashed hundreds of billions of dollars in direct payments to families. Donald Trump, not known as a paragon of compassion, has put a moratorium on foreclosures and evictions. Certainly one can take a cynical view of both these developments; nonetheless, they embody the principle of caring for the vulnerable.

From all over the world we hear stories of solidarity and healing. One friend described sending $100 each to ten strangers who were in dire need. My son, who until a few days ago worked at Dunkin' Donuts, said people were tipping at five times the normal rate—and these are working-class people, many of them Hispanic truck drivers, who are economically insecure themselves. Doctors, nurses, and "essential workers" in other professions risk their lives to serve the public. Here are some more examples of the love and kindness eruption, from an email from the philanthropic organization ServiceSpace:

Perhaps we're in the middle of living into that new story. Imagine Italian airforce using Pavarotti, Spanish military doing acts of service, and street police playing guitars—to *inspire*. Corporations giving unexpected wage hikes. Canadians starting "Kindness Mongering." Six year old in Australia adorably gifting her tooth fairy money, an 8th grader in Japan making 612 masks, and college kids everywhere buying groceries for elders. Cuba sending an army in "white robes" (doctors) to help Italy. A landlord allowing tenants to stay without rent, an Irish priest's poem going viral, disabled activists producing hand sanitizer. Imagine. Sometimes a crisis mirrors our deepest impulse—that we can always respond with compassion.

As Rebecca Solnit describes in her marvelous book, *A Paradise Built in Hell*, disaster often liberates solidarity. A more beautiful world shimmers just beneath the surface, bobbing up whenever the systems that hold it underwater loosen their grip.

For a long time we, as a collective, have stood helpless in the face of an ever-sickening society. Whether it is declining health, decaying infrastructure, depression, suicide, addiction, ecological degradation, or concentration of wealth, the symptoms of civilizational malaise in the developed world are plain to see, but we have been stuck in the systems and patterns that cause them. Now, Covid has gifted us a reset.

A million forking paths lie before us. Universal basic income could mean an end to economic insecurity and the flowering of creativity as millions are freed from the work that Covid has shown us is less necessary than we thought. Or it could mean, with the decimation of small businesses, dependency on the state for a stipend that comes with strict conditions. The crisis could usher in totalitarianism or solidarity;

medical martial law or a holistic renaissance; greater fear of the microbial world, or greater resiliency in participation in it; permanent norms of social distancing, or a renewed desire to come together.

What can guide us, as individuals and as a society, as we walk the garden of forking paths? At each junction, we can be aware of what we follow: fear or love, self-preservation or generosity. Shall we live in fear and build a society based on it? Shall we live to preserve our separate selves? Shall we use the crisis as a weapon against our political enemies? These are not all-or-nothing questions, all fear or all love. It is that a next step into love lies before us. It feels daring, but not reckless. It treasures life, while accepting death. And it trusts that with each step, the next will become visible.

Please don't think that choosing love over fear can be accomplished solely through an act of will, and that fear too can be conquered like a virus. The virus we face here is fear, whether it is fear of Covid-19 or fear of the totalitarian response to it, and this virus too has its terrain. Fear, along with addiction, depression, and a host of physical ills, flourishes in a terrain of separation and trauma: inherited trauma, childhood trauma, violence, war, abuse, neglect, shame, punishment, poverty, and the muted, normalized trauma that affects nearly everyone who lives in a monetized economy, undergoes modern schooling, or lives without community or connection to place. This terrain can be changed, by trauma healing on a personal level, by systemic change toward a more compassionate society, and by transforming the basic narrative of separation: the separate self in a world of other, me separate from you, humanity separate from nature. To be alone is a primal fear, and modern society has rendered us more and more alone. But the time of Reunion is here. Every act of compassion, kindness, courage, or generosity heals us from the story of separation, because it assures both actor and witness that we are in this together.

I will conclude by invoking one more dimension of the relationship between humans and viruses. Viruses are integral to evolution, not just of humans but of all eukaryotes. Viruses can transfer DNA from organism to organism, sometimes inserting it into the germline (where it becomes heritable).[15] Known as horizontal gene transfer, this is a primary mechanism of evolution, allowing life to evolve together much faster than is possible through random mutation. As Lynn Margulis once put it, we are our viruses.[16]

And now let me venture into speculative territory. Perhaps the great diseases of civilization have quickened our biological and cultural evolution, bestowing key genetic information and offering both individual and collective initiation. Could the current pandemic be just that? Novel RNA codes are spreading from human to human, imbuing us with new genetic information; at the same time, we are receiving other, esoteric "codes" that ride the back of the biological ones, disrupting our narratives and systems in the same way that an illness disrupts bodily physiology. The phenomenon follows the template of initiation: separation from normality, followed by a dilemma, breakdown, or ordeal, followed (if it is to be complete) by reintegration and celebration.

Now the question arises: Initiation into what? What is the specific nature and purpose of this initiation? The popular name for the pandemic offers a clue: coronavirus. A corona is a crown. "Novel Coronavirus pandemic" means "a new coronation for all."

Already we can feel the power of who we might become. A true sovereign does not run in fear from life or from death. A true sovereign does not dominate and conquer (that is a shadow archetype, the Tyrant). The true sovereign serves the people, serves life, and respects the sovereignty of all people. The coronation marks the emergence of the unconscious into consciousness, the crystallization of chaos into order, the transcendence of compulsion into choice. We become the rulers of that which had ruled us. The New World Order that the conspiracy theorists fear is a shadow of the glorious possibility available to sovereign beings. No longer the vassals of fear, we can bring order to the kingdom and build an intentional society on the love already shining through the cracks of the world of separation.

The Conspiracy Myth

MAY 2020

The accusations that I am a conspiracy theorist that followed the publication of "The Coronation" prompted me to write the following essay laying out how I think about conspiracy theories. It develops ideas I originally explored in an earlier essay titled "Synchronicity, Myth, and the New World Order."

As you will read, I offer an alternative to the true or false, prove or debunk thinking that characterizes the debate on the topic. Consequently, neither side was very happy with this essay. Those who think there is proof of conspiracy (to create Covid deliberately as an instrument of totalitarian takeover) thought I had my head in the sand. Those on the mainstream side thought I was being way too generous to conspiracy mongers who deserve nothing more than ridicule.

I am not ruling out the possibility that someday at least some of the conspiracy theories surrounding Covid will be accepted as true. Conspiracies do happen, and plausible means and motives are present. However, at present I still believe that most of the Covid response can be explained in other ways, namely systemic bias, groupthink, religious hysteria, mob mentality, and so forth—subjects from which conspiracy theories can divert much-needed attention.

On the other hand, the existence of other explanations does not obviate conspiracy. Conspiracies can coexist with and even exploit these phenomena. But even if shocking conspiracies are soon revealed, let us not ignore the conditions that enable them.

As I reread the essay, I remember another intention that I'd worked into it: I wanted to defuse the alarming authoritarian tactic of smearing Covid dissent as "right wing." Obviously my attempt was not successful: At the present writing in February 2022, Canadian prime minister, Justin Trudeau, and the mass media are slandering the truckers' convoy protesting vaccine mandates in exactly this way. More than a political tactic to quash dissent, it also bespeaks a collapse of traditional political categories, which itself is part of the breakdown of sense and meaning in the Covid era.

The other day I was amused to read a critique of "The Coronation" in which the author was absolutely certain that I am a closet conspiracy theorist. He was so persuasive that I myself almost believed it.

What is a conspiracy theory anyway? Sometimes the term *conspiracy theorist* is deployed against anyone who questions authority, dissents from dominant paradigms, or thinks that hidden interests influence our leading institutions. As such, this accusation is a way to quash dissent and bully those trying to stand up to abuses of power. One needn't abandon critical thinking to believe that powerful institutions sometimes collude, conspire, cover up, and are corrupt. If that is what is meant by a conspiracy theory, obviously some of those theories are true. Does anyone remember Enron? Iran-Contra? COINTELPRO? Vioxx? Iraqi weapons of mass destruction (WMD)?

During the time of Covid-19, another level of conspiracy theory has risen to prominence that goes way beyond specific stories of collusion and corruption to posit conspiracy as a core explanatory principle for how the world works. Fueled by the authoritarian response to the pandemic (justifiable or not, lockdown, quarantine, surveillance and tracking, censorship of misinformation, suspension of freedom of assembly and other civil liberties, and so on are indeed authoritarian), this arch-conspiracy theory holds that an evil, power-hungry cabal of insiders deliberately created the pandemic or at least ruthlessly exploited it to frighten the public into accepting a totalitarian world government under permanent medical martial law, a New World Order (NWO). Furthermore, this evil group, this Illuminati, pulls the strings of all major governments, corporations, the United Nations, the WHO, the CDC, the media, the intelligence services, the banks, and nongovernmental organizations (NGOs). In other words, they say, everything we are told is a lie, and the world is in the grip of evil.

So what do I think about that theory? I think it is a myth. And what is a myth? A myth is not the same thing as a fantasy or a delusion. Myths are vehicles of truth, and that truth needn't be literal. The classical Greek myths, for example, seem like mere amusements until one decodes them by associating each god with psychosocial forces. In this way, myths bring light to the shadows and reveal what has been repressed. They take a truth about the psyche or society and form it into a story. The truth of a myth does not depend on whether it is objectively verifiable. That is one reason why, in "The Coronation," I said my purpose was neither to advocate nor to debunk the conspiracy narrative, but rather to look at what it illuminates. It is, after all, neither provable nor falsifiable.

What is true about the conspiracy myth? Underneath its literalism, it conveys important information that we ignore at great peril.

First, it demonstrates the shocking extent of public alienation from institutions of authority. For all the political battles of the post–WWII era, there was at least a broad consensus on basic facts and on where facts could be found. The key institutions of knowledge production—science and journalism—enjoyed broad public trust. If the *New York Times* and the *CBS Evening News* said that North Vietnam attacked the United States in the Gulf of Tonkin, most people believed it. If science said nuclear power and DDT were safe, most people believed that, too. To some extent, that trust was well earned. Journalists sometimes defied the interests of the powerful, as with Seymour Hersh's exposé of the My Lai Massacre during the Vietnam War, or Woodward and Bernstein's reporting on Watergate. Science, in the vanguard of civilization's onward march, had a reputation for the objective pursuit of knowledge in defiance of traditional religious authorities, as well as a reputation for lofty disdain for political and financial motives.

Today, the broad consensus of trust in science and journalism is in tatters. I know several highly educated people who believe Earth is flat. By dismissing flat-earthers and the tens of millions of adherents to less extreme alternative narratives (historical, medical, political, and scientific) as ignorant, we are mistaking symptom for cause. Their loss of trust is a clear symptom of a loss of *trustworthiness*. Our institutions of knowledge production have betrayed public trust repeatedly, as have our political institutions. Now, many people won't believe them even when they tell the truth. This must be frustrating to the scrupulous doctor, scientist, or public official. To them, the problem looks like a public gone mad, a rising tide of antiscientific irrationality that is endangering public health. The solution, from that perspective, would be to combat ignorance. It is almost as if ignorance is a virus (in fact, I have heard that phrase before) that must be controlled through the same kind of quarantine (for example, censorship) that we apply to the coronavirus.

Ironically, another kind of ignorance pervades both these efforts: the ignorance of the terrain. What is the diseased tissue upon which the virus of ignorance gains purchase? The loss of trust in science, journalism, and government reflects their long corruption: their arrogance and elitism, their alliance with corporate interests, and their institutionalized suppression of dissent. The conspiracy myth embodies the realization of a profound disconnect between the public postures of our leaders and their true motivations and plans. It bespeaks a political culture that is opaque to the ordinary citizen, a world of secrecy, image, PR, spin, optics, talking points, perception management, narrative management, and information warfare. No wonder people suspect that there is another reality operating behind the curtains.

Second, the conspiracy myth gives narrative form to an authentic intuition that an inhuman power governs the world. What could that power be? The conspiracy myth locates that power in a group of malevolent human beings (who take commands, in some versions, from extraterrestrial or demonic entities). Therein lies a certain psychological comfort, because now there is someone to blame in a familiar us-versus-them narrative and victim-perpetrator-rescuer psychology. Alternatively, we could locate the "inhuman power" in systems or ideologies, not a group of conspirators. That is less psychologically rewarding, because we can no longer easily identify as heroes fighting evil; after all, we ourselves participate in these systems, which pervade our entire society. Systems like the debt-based money system, patriarchy, white supremacy, or capitalism cannot be removed by fighting their administrators. They create roles for evildoers to fill, but the evildoers are functionaries; puppets, not puppet masters. The basic intuition of conspiracy theories then is true: that those we think hold power are but puppets of the real power in the world.

A couple weeks ago I was on a call with a person who had a high position in the Obama administration and who still runs in elite circles. He said, "There is no one driving the bus." I was a little disappointed actually, because there is indeed part of me that wishes the problem were a bunch of dastardly conspirators. Why? Because then our world's problems would be quite easy to solve, at least in principle: Just expose and eliminate those bad guys. That is the prevailing Hollywood formula for righting the world's wrongs: A heroic champion confronts and defeats the bad guy, and everyone lives happily ever after. Hmm, that is the same basic formula as blaming ill health on germs and killing them with the arsenal of medicine, so that we can live safe, healthy lives ever after . . . or killing the terrorists or walling out the immigrants or locking up the criminals—all so that we can live safe, healthy lives ever after. Stamped from the same template, conspiracy theories tap into an unconscious orthodoxy. They emanate from the same mythic pantheon as the social ills they protest. We might call that pantheon Separation, and one of its chief motifs is the war against the Other.

That is not to say there is no such thing as a germ—or a conspiracy. Watergate, COINTELPRO, Iran-Contra, Merck's drug Vioxx, Ford's exploding Pinto cover-up, Lockheed Martin's bribery campaign, Bayer's knowing sale of HIV-contaminated blood, and the Enron scandal demonstrate that conspiracies involving powerful elites do happen. None of these conspiracies are myths though: A myth is something that explains the world; it is, mysteriously, bigger than itself. Thus, the Kennedy assassination conspiracy theory (some form of which I will confess, doubtless at cost to my credibility, to accepting as literally true) is a portal to the mythic realm. Even in its official rendition, the story and its characters have the quality of being larger than life.

The conspiracy myth I'm addressing here, though, is much larger than any of these specific examples: It says that the world as we know it is the result of a conspiracy, with the Illuminati or controllers as its evil gods. For believers, it becomes a totalizing discourse that casts every event into its terms.

It is a myth with an illustrious pedigree, going back at least to the time of the first-century Gnostics, who believed that an evil demiurge created the material world out of a preexisting divine essence. Creating the world in the image of his own distortion, the demiurge imagines himself to be its true god and ruler.

One needn't believe in this literally, nor believe literally in a world-controlling evil cabal, to derive insight from this myth—insight into the arrogance of the powerful, for example, or into the nature of the distortion that colors the world of our experience.

What is it that makes the vast majority of humanity comply with a system that drives Earth and humankind to ruin? What power has us in its grip? It isn't just the conspiracy theorists who are captive to a mythology. Society at large is, too. I call it the mythology of Separation: me separate from you, matter separate from spirit, human separate from nature. It holds us as discrete and separate selves in an objective universe of force and mass, atoms and void. Because we are (in this myth) separate from other people and from nature, we must dominate our competitors and master nature. Progress, therefore, consists in increasing our capacity to control the Other. The myth recounts human history as an ascent from one triumph to the next, from fire to domestication to industry to information technology, genetic engineering, and social science, promising a coming paradise of control. That same myth motivates the conquest and ruin of nature, organizing society to turn the entire planet into money—no conspiracy necessary.

The mythology of Separation is what generates what I named in "The Coronation" as a civilizational tilt toward control. The solution template is, facing any problem, to find something to control—to quarantine, to track, to imprison, to wall out, to dominate, or to kill. If control fails, more control will fix it. To achieve social and material paradise, control everything, track every movement, monitor every word, record every transaction. Then there can be no more crime, no more infection, no more disinformation. When the entire ruling class accepts this formula and this vision, they will act in natural concert to increase their control. It is all for the greater good. When the public accepts it, too, they will not resist it. This is not a conspiracy, though it can certainly look like one. This is a third truth within the conspiracy myth. Events are indeed orchestrated in the direction of more and more control, only the orchestrating power is itself a zeitgeist, an ideology . . . a myth.

A Conspiracy with No Conspirators

Let us not dismiss the conspiracy myth as *just* a myth. Not only is it an important psychosocial diagnostic, but it reveals what is otherwise hard to see from the official mythology in which society's main institutions, while flawed, are shepherding us ever-closer to a high tech paradise. That dominant myth blinds us to the data points the conspiracy theorists recruit for their narratives. These might include things like regulatory capture in the pharmaceutical industry, conflicts of interest within public health organizations, the dubious efficacy of masks, the far-lower-than-hyped death rates, totalitarian overreach, the questionable utility of lockdowns, concerns about nonionizing frequencies of electromagnetic radiation, the benefits of natural and holistic approaches to boosting immunity, bioterrain theory, the dangers of censorship in the name of "combating disinformation," and so forth. It would be nice if one could raise the numerous valid points and legitimate questions that alternative Covid narratives bring to light without being classed as a right-wing conspiracy theorist.

The whole phrase "right-wing conspiracy theorist" is a bit odd, since traditionally it is the Left that has been most alert to the proclivity of the powerful to abuse their power. Traditionally, it is the Left that is suspicious of corporate interests, that urges us to "question authority," and that has in fact been the main victim of government infiltration and surveillance. Fifty years ago, if anyone said, "There is a secret program called COINTELPRO that is spying on civil rights groups and sowing division within them with poison pen letters and fabricated rumors," that would have been a conspiracy theory by today's standards. The same, twenty-five years ago, with, "There is a secret program in which the CIA facilitates narcotics sales into American inner cities and uses the money to fund right-wing paramilitaries in Central America." The same with government infiltration of environmental groups and peace activists starting in the 1980s. Or more recently, the coordinated infiltration by law enforcement and corporate interests of the Standing Rock pipeline protest.[1] Or the real estate industry's decades-long conspiracy to redline neighborhoods to keep black people out. Given this history, why all of a sudden is it the Left urging everyone to trust "the Man"—to trust the pronouncements of the pharmaceutical companies and pharma-funded organizations like the CDC and WHO? Why is skepticism toward these institutions labeled "right wing"? It isn't as if only the privileged are "inconvenienced" by lockdown. It is devastating the lives of tens or hundreds of millions of the global precariat. The UN World Food Programme is warning that by the end of the year, 260 million people will face starvation.[2] Most are black and brown people in Africa and South Asia. One might argue that to restrict the debate to epidemiological questions of mortality is itself a privileged stance that erases the suffering of those who are most marginalized to begin with.

"Conspiracy theory" has become a term of political invective, used to disparage any view that diverges from mainstream beliefs. Basically, any critique of dominant institutions can be smeared as conspiracy theory. There is actually a perverse truth in this smear. For example, if you believe that glyphosate is actually dangerous to human and ecological health, then you also must, if you are logical, believe that Bayer/Monsanto is suppressing or ignoring that information, and you must also believe that the government, media, and scientific establishment are to some extent complicit in that suppression. Otherwise, why are we not seeing *New York Times* headlines like "Monsanto Whistleblower Reveals Dangers of Glyphosate"?

Information suppression can happen without deliberate orchestration. Throughout history, hysterias, intellectual fads, and mass delusions have come and gone spontaneously. This is more mysterious than the easy conspiracy explanation admits. An unconscious coordination of action can look very much like a conspiracy, and the boundary between the two is blurry. Consider the weapons of mass destruction (WMD) fraud that served as a pretext for the US invasion of Iraq in 2003. Maybe there were people in the Bush administration who knowingly used the phony "yellowcake" document to call for war; maybe they just wanted very much to believe the documents were genuine, or maybe they thought, "Well, this is questionable but Saddam Hussein must have WMD, and even if he doesn't, he wants them, so the document is basically true . . ." People easily believe what serves their interests or fits their existing worldview.

In a similar vein, the media needed little encouragement to start beating the war drums. They knew what to do already, without having to receive instructions. I don't think very many journalists actually believed the WMD lie. They pretended to believe, because subconsciously they knew that was the establishment narrative. That was what would get them recognized as serious journalists. That's what would give them access to power. That is what would allow them to keep their jobs and advance their careers. But most of all, they pretended to believe because everyone else was pretending to believe. It is hard to go against the zeitgeist.

The British scientist Rupert Sheldrake told me about a talk he gave to a group of scientists who were working on animal behavior at a prestigious British university. He was talking about his research on dogs that knew when their owners were coming home, and other telepathic phenomena in domestic animals. The talk was received with a kind of polite silence. But in the following tea break all six of the senior scientists who were present at the seminar came to him one by one, and when they were sure that no one else was listening told him they had had experiences of this kind with their own animals, or that they were convinced that telepathy is a real phenomenon, but that they could not talk to their colleagues about this because they were all so straight.

When Sheldrake realized that all six had told him much the same thing, he said to them, "Why don't you guys come out? You'd all have so much more fun!" He says that when he gives a talk at a scientific institution there are nearly always scientists who approach him afterward telling him they've had personal experiences that convince them of the reality of psychic or spiritual phenomena but that they can't discuss them with their colleagues for fear of being thought weird.

This is not a deliberate conspiracy to suppress psychic phenomena. Those six scientists didn't convene beforehand and decide to suppress information they knew was real. They keep their opinions to themselves because of the norms of their subculture, the basic paradigms that delimit science, and the very real threat of damage to their careers. The persecution and calumny directed at Sheldrake himself demonstrates what happens to a scientist who is outspoken in his dissent from official scientific reality. So we might still say that a conspiracy is afoot, but its perpetrator is a culture, a system, and a story.

Is this, or a deliberate conspiratorial agenda, a more satisfying explanation for the seemingly inexorable trends (which by no means began with Covid) toward surveillance, tracking, distancing, germ phobia, obsession with safety, and the digitization and indoor-ization of entertainment, recreation, and sociality? If the perpetrator is indeed a cultural mythology and system, then conspiracy theories offer us a false target, a distraction. The remedy cannot be to expose and take down those who have foisted these trends upon us. Of course, there are many bad actors in our world, remorseless people committing heinous acts. But have they created the system and the mythology of Separation, or do they merely take advantage of it? Certainly such people should be stopped, but if that is all we do, and leave unchanged the conditions that breed them, we will fight an endless war. Just as in bioterrain theory where germs are the symptoms and exploiters of diseased tissue, so also are conspiratorial cabals the symptoms and exploiters of a diseased society: a society poisoned by the mentality of war, fear, separation, and control. This deep ideology, the myth of separation, is beyond anyone's power to invent. The Illuminati, if they exist, are not its authors; it is more true to say that the mythology is their author. We do not create our myths; they create us.

Which Side Are You On?

In the end, I still haven't said whether I think the New World Order conspiracy myth is true or not. Well actually, yes, I have. I have said it is true as a myth, regardless of its correspondence to verifiable facts. But what about the facts? Come on, Charles, tell us: Is there actually a conspiracy behind the Covid thing, or isn't there? There must be an objective fact of the matter. Are chemtrails a thing? Was SARS-CoV-2 genetically engineered? Is microwave radiation from cell phone towers a factor in Covid? Are vaccines introducing viruses from animal cell cultures into people? Is Bill Gates masterminding a power grab in the form of medical martial law? Does a Luciferian elite rule the world? True or false? Yes or no?

To these questions I would respond with another: Given that I am not an expert on any of these matters, why do you want to know what I think? Could it be to place me on one side or another of an information war? Then you will know whether it is okay to enjoy this essay, share it, or have me on your podcast. In an us-versus-them war mentality, the most important thing is to know which side someone is on, lest you render aid and comfort to the enemy.

Aha—Charles must be on the other side. Because he has created a false equivalency between peer-reviewed, evidence-based, respectable scientific knowledge on the one hand, and unhinged conspiracy theories on the other.

Aha—Charles must be on the other side. Because he has created a false equivalency between corporate-government-NWO propaganda on the one hand, and brave whistleblowers and dissidents risking their careers for the truth on the other.

Can you see how totalizing war mentality can be?

War mentality saturates our polarized society, which envisions progress as a consequence of victory—victory over a virus, over the ignorant, over the Left, over the Right, over the psychopathic elites, over Donald Trump, over white supremacy, over the liberal elites. . . . Each side uses the same formula, and that formula requires an enemy. So, obligingly, we divide ourselves up into us and them, exhausting 99 percent of our energies in a fruitless tug-of-war, never once suspecting that the true evil power might be the formula itself.

This is not to propose that we somehow banish conflict from human affairs. It is to question a mythology—embraced by both sides—that conceives every problem in conflict's terms. Struggle and conflict have their place, but other plotlines are possible. There are other pathways to healing and to justice.

A Call for Humility

Have you ever noticed that events seem to organize themselves to validate the story you hold about the world? Selection bias and confirmation bias explain some of that, but I think something weirder is at work, as well. When we enter into deep faith or deep paranoia, it seems as if that state attracts confirmatory events to it. Reality organizes itself to match our stories. In a sense, this *is* a conspiracy, just not one perpetrated by humankind. That might be a third truth that the conspiracy myth harbors: the presence of an organizing intelligence behind the events of our lives.

In no way does this imply the New Age nostrum that beliefs create reality. Rather, it is that reality and belief construct each other, coevolving as a coherent whole. The intimate, mysterious connection between myth and reality means that belief is never actually a slave to fact. We are facts' sovereign—which is not to say their creator. To be their sovereign doesn't mean to be their tyrant, disrespecting and overruling them. The wise monarch pays attention to an unruly subject, such as a fact that defies the narrative. Maybe it is simply a disturbed troublemaker, like a simple lie, but maybe it signals disharmony in the kingdom. Maybe the kingdom is no longer legitimate. Maybe the myth is no longer true. It could well be that the vociferous attacks on Covid dissent, using the "conspiracy theory" smear, signal the infirmity of the orthodox paradigms they seek to uphold.

If so, that doesn't mean the orthodox paradigms are all wrong, either. To leap from one certainty to another skips the holy ground of uncertainty, of not knowing, of humility, into which genuinely new information can come. What unites the pundits of all persuasions is their certainty. Who is trustworthy? In the end, it is the person with the humility to recognize when he or she has been wrong.

To those who categorically dismiss any information that seriously challenges conventional medicine, lockdown policies, vaccines, and so forth, I would ask, Do you need such high walls around your kingdom? Instead of banishing these unruly subjects, would it hurt to give them an audience? Would it be so dangerous to perhaps tour another kingdom, guided not by your own loyal minister but by the most intelligent, welcoming partisans of the other side? If you have no interest in spending the several hours it will take to absorb the following dissenting opinions, fine. I'd rather be in my garden, too. But if you are a partisan in these issues, what harm will it do to visit enemy territory? Normally partisans don't do that. They rely on the reports from their own leaders about the enemy. If they know anything of Robert F. Kennedy Jr.'s or Judy Mikovits's views, it is through the lens of someone debunking them. So give a listen to Kennedy, or if you prefer MDs only, to David Katz, Zach Bush, or Christiane Northrup.

I would like to offer the same invitation to those who reject the conventional view. Find the most scrupulous mainstream doctors and scientists you can, and dive into their world. Take the attitude of a respectful guest, not a hostile spy. If you do that, I guarantee you will encounter data points that challenge any narrative you came in with. The splendor of conventional virology, the wonders of chemistry that generations of scientists have discovered, the intelligence and sincerity of most of these scientists, and the genuine altruism of health care workers on the front line who have no political or financial conflict of interest in the face of grave risk to themselves, must be part of any satisfactory narrative.

After two months of obsessively searching for one, I have not yet found a satisfactory narrative that can account for every data point. That doesn't mean to take no action because, after all, knowledge is never certain. But in the whirlwind of competing narratives and the disjoint mythologies beneath them, we can look for action that makes sense no matter which side is right. We can look for truths that the smoke and clamor of the battle obscures. We can question assumptions both sides take for granted, and ask questions neither side is asking. Not identified with either side, we can gather knowledge from both. Generalizing to society, by bringing in all the voices, including the marginalized ones, we can build a broader social consensus and begin to heal the polarization that is rending and paralyzing our society.

Numb

JULY 2020

This essay amplifies some of the themes from "The Coronation" and focuses particularly on a question I apply to many other fields, particularly money and climate change: What do our metrics leave out? The girl's video I reference here is testimony to a human cost to lockdowns that never figured in epidemiologists' cost-benefit analyses. To be sure, after two years of pandemic measures we are beginning to see academic studies of their impact on child development and emotional well-being, confirming what many of us knew from the outset. Yet to this day, "saving lives" diminishes other values in discussion of Covid policy. Shall we grant the premise that society's primary guideline for making decisions is how many deaths we can postpone?

At the time of its writing, we were still being told that lockdown and distancing measures were temporary, just to "flatten the curve." Okay, they had gone on more than the two or three weeks originally advertised, but it was still to be a temporary state of affairs. That essay was doubtful, warning of mutations (what are now called variants) that could extend the Covid public health regime indefinitely. This has indeed come to pass in most countries, interrupted with temporary, partial rollbacks. Now that the precedent is set and the enforcement

technology developed, we might expect that it is freedom that is
temporary. Unless we the people choose otherwise.

T he title of this essay, "Numb," comes from a heartbreaking
three-minute film made by a teenage girl, Liv McNeil.[1]
Simply yet precisely crafted, it documents the withering of a
teenager's life in the time of Covid lockdown. The camera lingers
over photographs of her having fun with her friends. Then onto
her computer screen, her assignments, scrolling, scrolling . . . her
life now held in a box. And then scores of still shots of herself
sitting on her bed, day after day, trying to stay upbeat as her
patience gradually gives way to numbness.

I shared the video with a close friend who related a similar
story about her own teenage daughter, whom I'll call Sarah. A
vivacious, spirited, outgoing girl, who was often outdoors and
rarely looked at screens, she "wilted like a flower cut off at the
roots," becoming sad and listless. Fortunately, my friend, who
is relatively wealthy, found Sarah an opportunity to work with
horses and life came back to her.

I am happy for Sarah, but what of all the less lucky ones spending endless hours in their bedrooms, motionless, staring at the
screen, socializing in but two dimensions, starving for the society
of their friends? No more sleepovers, no more choir, no more
theater, no more sports, no more parties, no more outings, no
more dances, no more summer camp, no more band practice . . .

Before I go on, let me pause to give voice to what many readers
must be thinking: "Quit your over-privileged complaining! What
is the sacrifice of play and sociality compared to saving lives?"

I agree that protecting people's health is important, yet its value
must stand alongside other values. To see that it is a relative and
not an absolute value, consider a hypothetical extreme in which
we could save one life by locking down all society for a year. I don't
think many people would agree to that. On the other extreme,

imagine we were faced with a plague with a 90 percent mortality rate. In that case, few would resist the most stringent lockdown measures. Covid-19 is obviously somewhere in between.

In modern society, saving lives is a paramount value. (Actually the term is a misnomer—there is no such thing as saving a life, since we are mortal and will all one day die. Therefore let us use a more accurate phrase: postponing deaths.) Much of public discourse, from health care to foreign policy, revolves around safety, security, and risk. Covid-19 policy also centers on how to prevent as many deaths as possible and how to keep people safe. Values such as the immeasurable benefits of children's play, of singing or dancing together, of physical touch and human togetherness are not part of the calculations. Why?

One reason is simply that these immeasurables elude calculation, and therefore fit poorly into a policy-making process that prides itself on being scientific; that is, quantitative, based on the numbers. But I think there is a deeper reason, rooted in modern civilization's conception of who we are and why we are here. What is the purpose of life? What is it, even, to be alive?

I have written in an earlier essay about the mania for safety, the denial of death, the glorification of youth, and the all-encompassing program of control that has engulfed our society. Here I will state a simple truth: There is more to living than merely staying alive. We are here to *live* life, not just survive life. That would be obvious if the certainty of death were integrated into our psychology, but in modern society, sadly, it is not. We hide death away. We live in a pretense of permanence. Seeking the impossible—the infinite postponement of death—we fail to fully live life.

We are not the discrete, separate individuals that modernity narrates to us. We are interconnected. We are inter-existent. We are relationship. To live fully means to relate fully. Covid-19 is a further step in a long trend of disconnection from community, from nature, and from place. With each step of disconnection, although we may survive as separate selves, we become less and less alive. The young and the old are especially sensitive to this disconnection. We see them shrivel like fruit in a drought. As a psychiatrist friend recently wrote to me, "Among the elderly, the fallout has been truly disastrous. Being quarantined in the room and isolated from family is causing massive amounts of invisible suffering and decline, as well as deaths. I can't tell you how many anguished family members have told me that it's not Covid that is killing their loved one—it's the restrictions."

I am not advocating that sociality become a new absolutism to replace death postponement as the overriding determinant of public policy. I just want it to be prominent in the conversation. I want to enshrine it as a sacred value. A full social life is not some privileged add-on to the meeting of measurable physical needs, it is a basic human right and a basic human necessity. This is not just a problem of privilege either; if anything, isolation afflicts the poor even more than the affluent, since the poor have less access to the technological substitutes—pallid though they are—for in-person community. Furthermore, what right have we to say that the degree of suffering is less from loneliness than it is from hunger or disease? When loneliness drives people to stop eating, to loll listlessly day after day, even to attempt suicide, it is profound suffering indeed.

The final irony is that in the end, a policy based on minimizing deaths won't even achieve that. Life withers in isolation. This is true on a biological level, as we require ongoing intercourse with the world of microbes and, yes, viruses, to maintain bodily equilibrium. It is true as well on the social level: one prominent meta-analytic review concluded that social isolation, loneliness, and living alone cause an average of 29 percent, 26 percent, and 32 percent increased likelihood of mortality, respectively.[2] That's roughly the same risk level as smoking fifteen cigarettes a day or habitual excessive drinking. But I have not seen our politicians or medical authorities including such considerations in their epidemiologically informed policy decisions.

But that isn't what I am protesting here. Even if this ironic failure weren't so, even if we could postpone death forever by isolating each person in a bubble, it still wouldn't be worth it. I know that when I watch "Numb." I know that when I see my own children doing their best to cope in a socially impoverished landscape; when my older sons speak of loneliness, apathy, and depression; when my fifteen-year-old sees his friends through screens or, very occasionally, through masks and six feet apart; when my youngest begs constantly for a "playdate." What are we doing to our children? Will no one stand up for the value of a game of tag? A gaggle of kids piling all over each other? I can't put a number on the value of these activities compared to postponing X number of deaths. I just know that they are far more important than society has made them.

Some might say this is only temporary, life will go back to normal as soon as we have a vaccine. Well, even ardent vaccine proponents like Bill Gates are saying that these vaccines will offer only temporary protection. Besides, there may be new mutations, new influenza pandemics, or some other disease. As long as we hold death postponement as our highest priority, there will always be reasons to keep the children locked down. We are today setting a precedent and establishing what is normal and acceptable.

While most people don't have access to an internship at a horse farm, the basic principle is widely practicable. It is the principle of reconnection. The migration of childhood onto screens and the indoors did not start with Covid, nor did the rise of childhood depression, anxiety, and other disorders. In particular, the disabled and neurodiverse have often lived with the degree of isolation that children (and the rest of us) are experiencing en masse. Now we have a wake-up call to reverse this trend both in our parenting and in our public policy—to revalue play, outdoors, connection to place, interaction with nature, and community gathering.

Many people have died or suffered permanent impairment from Covid-19. I offer my sincere condolences to them and their families. And I would like also to offer my condolences to the young people for the lost months of play, friendship, and gathering. It is not supposed to be this way, certainly not for long. These are not conditions suitable for your thriving; if you feel confined, listless, or depressed, it is not your fault. My heart goes out to you. But our sympathies are not enough. It is up to us adults to see the suffering that Liv McNeil has helped make visible, bring it into the public conversation, and do something about it. There is more to parenting than keeping our children safe.

The Banquet of Whiteness

AUGUST 2020

When I wrote this essay in August 2020, I noticed a narrative was forming that to question Covid orthodoxy was to engage in white supremacy. The argument was that people of color were dying in disproportionate numbers from Covid; therefore, if you stood in the way of current public health measures, you were harming those disadvantaged people. The argument is circular on its face, asserting its own premises (that the measures are effective, that there is no better response) as proof of its conclusion. Nonetheless, the race argument was vigorously employed to locate Covid dissent in the ugliest precincts of right-wing politics.

So I decided to look more closely at whiteness. If the term is to mean anything at all, it must include the systems of thought and knowledge that run Eurocentric civilization—including science and medicine. These have been part of the same colonial project that began with Christianity; in fact, science succeeded Christianity as the main replacement for indigenous belief systems.

"The Banquet of Whiteness" was completely ignored. It got fewer views and shares than almost anything else I've written. I think people just didn't know what to make of it. It sort of outflanked the Left on

the left, using its language and concepts to make a point contrary to its current political position on Covid. So the Left shunned it. So did the Right, who I imagine skip over anything that deploys the concept of "whiteness" in any way.

The essay was also motivated simply by my indignation at the way Dr. Stella Immanuel was treated, as I describe in the essay. The way that the media mob turned on her stimulated me to begin considering mob dynamics in general as a driver of Covid hysteria, a topic I took up in earnest in 2021.

Y ou may remember the affair of Dr. Stella Immanuel, now long buried under the detritus of the news cycle. I'd like to exhume it for a moment, as its remains reveal a hidden cultural racism that afflicts the supposedly anti-racist Left nearly as much as it does the traditional Right.

Dr. Immanuel, who hails from Cameroon and received her medical training in Nigeria, participated in a right-wing associated press conference in which a succession of medical doctors expressed dissenting views on Covid public policy. She described her clinical success treating Covid with a combination of zinc, Zithromax, and HCQ (hydroxychloroquine). The latter, of course, was tainted by its association with Donald Trump and has been virtually eliminated from the Covid pharmacopeia of the United States and many other Western countries. Dr. Immanuel also spoke of its wide use in Africa, where doctors are well familiar with it as a malarial drug, and admonished American doctors to trust that their colleagues in Africa are real doctors who wouldn't be using it if it didn't work.

I hold no strong opinion about HCQ, a chemical that clinical studies in the United States have shown to work quite well on Republicans. Joking aside, it is impossible to discern much about the drug through the haze of political pettifoggery that surrounds it, a haze that also obscures deeper issues than whether or not it is effective: issues around Big Pharma, the funding of medical research, and cultural imperialism.

Within hours the press conference was scrubbed from YouTube, Facebook, and Twitter, and the media descended upon the doctors with a furious vengeance, especially Dr. Immanuel. Here is a typical takedown from the website Daily Beast:

> Immanuel, a pediatrician and a religious minister, has a history of making bizarre claims about medical topics and other issues. She has often claimed that gynecological problems like cysts and endometriosis are in fact caused by people having sex in their dreams with demons and witches.
>
> She alleges alien DNA is currently used in medical treatments, and that scientists are cooking up a vaccine to prevent people from being religious. And, despite appearing in Washington, D.C. to lobby Congress on Monday, she has said that the government is run in part not by humans but by "reptilians" and other aliens.[1]

Other commentators dug up videos of Dr. Immanuel performing exorcisms to drive out evil spirits. Surely, the reasoning goes, we shouldn't listen to a person like this on matters of medical policy.

The racism of this criticism has little to do with the fact that its target happens to be black. Rather, it embodies a cultural superiority complex so entrenched that its precepts seem, to those immersed in it, like reality itself.

Let's look first at the "bizarre" idea that gynecological problems are caused by dream sex with demons and witches. In fact, such ideas are commonplace in indigenous and traditional cultures, the more general idea being that improper or unlucky interactions with the spirit world, ancestors, sorcerers, and the like can result in disease, injury, or financial misfortune. Accordingly, healers treat disease by exorcising bad spirits, lifting curses, negotiating with the ancestors, driving away ghosts, and so on.

People in those cultures widely consider such methods to be effective. Why do they believe in them? Here are two possibilities:

(1) Mired in ignorance and superstition, they have yet to emerge into the light of modern science, which would lay bare the absurdity of their primitive beliefs and usher them into the enlightened world of evidence, reason, and truth. They are less advanced than we are, and their progress is a matter of adopting our, superior, way of engaging the world.

(2) They believe in them because they work. Which means these people are no less intelligent, no less empirical, no less rational, and no less astute than we are.

Would you ridicule a Hindu villager for saying that the earth rests on the back of a turtle? Would you ridicule a Hopi or Diné for saying that Spider Grandmother weaves the world? Most of us know better than to do that, yet a shade of that ridicule colors the ready dismissal of other cultures' ideas of health and disease.

The Bizarre Other

A bit of personal history here. When I arrived in Taiwan in 1987, still a teenager, I found a culture in which beliefs and phenomena I considered bizarre were commonplace. People would hire *dangji* (Taiwanese for the Mandarin *jitong*, or shaman) and Taoist priests for all kinds of situations: illness, business problems, family problems, misfortune on a construction site, ghosts, and so on. People were generally satisfied with these services, and even highly educated people and large business enterprises would engage them (along with feng shui experts, astrologers, and so forth) when breaking ground, planning a wedding, or launching a business. Having already at that age been influenced by postcolonial thinking, I was loath to dismiss these practices out of hand, which would have required a patronizing certainty that my ways (of living and of knowing) were superior to theirs. I recognized such a dismissal to be part of a familiar colonial pattern of subjugation. Are we really so sure that our ways are the best ways?

The kind of exorcism that Dr. Immanuel performs, representing a syncretic overlay of Christianity on prior pantheistic worldviews, is only "bizarre" to the insular, culture-bound Western mind. The media have called Dr. Immanuel a "witch doctor," a "crazy," and in the words of a commentator on the now-defunct video-sharing website LiveLeak, a "religious lunatic voodoo priestess," who went to medical school in "Yes . . . *that* Nigeria" (presumably the Nigeria of internet scammers? Or from among Trump's "shithole countries"?).[2] The very use of the word *voodoo* as a term of disparagement illustrates my point, since voodoo exemplifies the rich syncretic traditions through which native peoples met the onslaught of colonialism and Christianity, appearing to have been converted but actually performing a reversal by incorporating the religion of the conqueror into their own culture. Anyone who uses the word *voodoo* to connote someone else's ignorance only demonstrates their own.

A similar disparaging tone infuses the mainstream media's treatment of other, non-Western treatments for Covid-19 (and non-Western medicines in general). Let's take for example traditional Chinese medicine (TCM), which has been used on over 90 percent of patients in China with Covid-19.[3] While the Chinese people and government are quite confident in the therapeutic effectiveness of the six main herbal formulas (some thousands of years old) used to treat Covid, the Western popular and scientific press know better. Here are some representative quotes:

> China is promoting coronavirus treatments based on unproven traditional medicines. . . .

For TCM, there is no good evidence, and therefore its use is not just unjustified, but dangerous.

—from *Nature*[4]

[TCM] can also give patients a false sense of security, leading them to neglect proven medications or therapies....

Herbal remedies—which China is exporting as part of its efforts to combat the coronavirus around the world—pose both direct and indirect risks to patients.

—from *NBC News* (subheadline: "But Scientists Warn Against It")[5]

A lack of standards and almost no clinical trials have hampered the widespread adoption of TCM....

Critics say China is now using the pandemic as a way to promote it [TCM] abroad.

—from the *BBC*[6]

If it took an attitude of cultural respect, the Western media wouldn't be so quick to write off a medical tradition with thousands of years of clinical experience and refinement practiced by literally hundreds of thousands of doctors. Chinese people alone make more than 2.5 billion visits to TCM doctors annually.[7] To imagine that they have somehow been in the grips of a collective mass delusion for thousands of years is a kind of lazy cultural arrogance. It is the mentality of, "They must not be as smart, as rational, as evidence-based as we are. Their advancement means to adopt our medicine. We can improve them by bringing our ways to them, because we know better than they do."

It would be an error to attribute the dismissal of TCM to overt racism. The Western medical establishment rejects TCM in large part because it is unwilling to seriously look at it in the first place. After all, how could anything match science? Furthermore, a cultural misapprehension of the basic philosophy of TCM reduces a sophisticated, coherent, and self-sufficient set of paradigms to a crude, haphazard corpus of placebo, superstition, and guesswork. This cultural superiority complex assumes that we in the West know better, that our standards of proof are higher, that we can see obvious flaws in reason and evidence that they cannot. Thus, the experts quoted in *Nature* and *NBC News* belittle TCM for "Using vague terms and nonpharmacological concepts or testing too many combinations of herbs to parse out their specific effects."[8] What are "nonpharmacological concepts"? Things like "wind heat," "spleen qi," or "liver fire." To the culturally bound Western scientific mind, these are nonsense. They are sensible only if one admits the possibility that another culture might apprehend the world as astutely and fruitfully as ourselves using an entirely different conceptual vocabulary. As for "too many combinations of herbs," this bespeaks an even more fundamental blindness. TCM is holistic and its formulas are irreducible. The whole is greater than the sum of its parts, because its herbal formulas are synergistic. The normal experimental method of isolating variables and identifying active ingredients (that can then become the basis of pharmaceutical drugs) is antithetical to TCM's basic diagnostics and therapies. As for a "lack of standards," that is because prescriptions and doses are tailored to the individual. The demand that TCM research abide by standardized and reductionistic practices is an act of cultural imperialism, justifiable if and only if our own culture's framework of knowledge is superior to theirs.

I could make similar points about African medicine(s). Although these may not have thousands of years of written history, they too arise from intelligent worldviews and systems of knowledge. Even scientifically trained African medical doctors like Dr. Immanuel might usefully draw on them in their medical thinking. Maybe that explains the popularity in much of Africa of *Artemisia annua,* or sweet wormwood, for treating Covid-19. Like HCQ, *Artemisia annua* is a malaria remedy, and it has been savagely suppressed by the pharmaceutical industry. (Watch the compelling film *The Malaria Business* produced by French public television.)[9] Also used in China for febrile diseases for thousands of years, it is banned in many countries on the pretext that it contains toxic components. Well, yes, if you go through its scores of active chemicals, you will find some that, in large, concentrated doses, will cause illness. (That is what was done to justify its prohibition.) In any event, the herb is on the radar today after the president of Madagascar (yes, *that* Madagascar) touted its efficacy in treating Covid-19. The Western media responded predictably with headlines like "Amid WHO Warnings and with No Proof, Some African Nations Turn to Herbal Tonic to Try to Treat Covid-19."[10] Oh, those backward Africans. The favorite term in headlines like this is "unproven." Also, "miracle cure" (a rabid mischaracterization—I've not read any accounts of actual Africans claiming that). I thought, of course it is "unproven," when herbal therapies lack the billions of dollars of research funding that go toward pharmaceuticals, and when the medical establishment is ignorant of how to use them or outright hostile to them. My point here is that this ignorance, this systemic and rhetorical belittling of herbal medicine, is also part of a cultural hegemony that spreads its scientistic gospel to the benighted with missionary zeal.

Ontological Imperialism

None of this is to say that modern medicine has nothing to offer traditional cultures. Indeed, Dr. Immanuel herself went to medical school, practices medicine in Texas, and advocates a combination of three modern pharmaceutical substances. This ability to operate in multiple realities or multiple mythologies is a central characteristic of nonmodern psychology. It stands in contrast to the ontological domination of "white" culture, which tells everyone else what is so and which either excludes other systems of knowledge, writes them off as superstition, tolerates them as anthropological subjects, assigns them a second-class metaphoric truth, or fetishizes them in the subtly patronizing category of "indigenous wisdom."

I put "white" in quotes here, because it has only an incidental relation to skin color, as any light-skinned Sami or other indigenous person would affirm. Yet there is also a sense of *whitewashing* here, a painting of the entire world in the pale tones of a single homogenizing paradigm. Furthermore, it happens to be light-skinned cultures that developed to its fullest degree the mythology of modernity and spread it around the world. Christian missionaries set the example that economic and scientific missionaries have followed.

So there are two levels of ontological imperialism running here. First is simply, "We're right and you're wrong." The second, more subtle level is, "Only one of us could possibly be right, as our views are in contradiction. It's either-or." But a Hindu might have no problem saying that the world rests on a turtle's back, and that it also originated by accretion of meteorites. Further, he might say this without relegating one to a realer status than the other—that the accretion disk is real and the turtle is metaphorical. Neither need dominate the other.

Can you see the kinship between ontological domination and other forms of domination (economic, political)? The habit of ontological domination is what might lead you to ask me, "But surely, Charles, you don't believe that demon sex can *actually* cause gynecological problems? Surely you don't believe that there is *actually* alien DNA in medical treatments or that reptilian ETs have *actually* infiltrated the government?" We as a culture are not well practiced in engaging multiple mythologies, of shifting from one to another as they become useful. It's worth pointing out that questions such as these encode ontological primacy in the word "actually."

71

To model another way, I would answer them like this: I do not normally operate in the world-story of witches, demons, aliens, and reptilians. I do not normally think in those terms. More often, though still not normally, do I think in terms of spleen qi or wind heat. Neither, though, do I disparage or dismiss any of these world-stories out of hand. I adopt an attitude of curiosity and respect. What is their power and what are their limitations? What does one become inhabiting them? What is gained and what is lost? What is it like to see the world in their terms? What thoughts and perceptions are available when speaking that language? I ask these same questions in engaging modern science and medicine.

This nonattachment to a standard, homogenizing world-story offers several advantages. First, one is able to avail oneself of the benefits of TCM or a competent neighborhood voodoo exorcist when modern medicine fails (because of its own configuration of "power and limitation"). I have in my life certainly benefited from all three (TCM most of all, but also an exorcism helped me once, and I am grateful to modern emergency dentistry, without which I'd probably be dead right now). Secondly, unattached to any One True Reality, one becomes less fearful of uncertainty and change, more adaptable, flexible, and resourceful. Third, one is able to engage people of other cultures and other world-stories respectfully, without the unavoidable patronizing racism of thinking you *know* better than they do. This is true respect. Respect is a willingness to be hosted in another's world, to honor their customs and learn their language. Today's contentious debates around cultural appropriation might dissolve if we understood the spirit of guest and host as we take a seat at each other's cultural banquets. If you have ever traveled abroad, you may have experienced how people appreciate even a feeble attempt to learn their local language. Respect opens the portal of welcome. The same is true for the language of beliefs.

Do not mistake this as an argument for the postmodern idea that truth is but a power-fraught cultural construct. There is a mysterious way in which it is true that the world rests on the back of a turtle, and in which it is not true that the Flying Spaghetti Monster created the world. Truth is discovered or revealed, not made.

Perhaps it is because it rings with truth that the World Turtle appears in numerous unrelated mythologies from India, China, and North America. As for primordial planetary accretion, there is significant disagreement among astronomers about how planets form. Just sayin'.

Now somebody can go edit my (already wildly inaccurate) Wikipedia page to say, "Eisenstein claims that the world really does rest on the back of a turtle."

Inclusion or Erasure?

A lot of ostensibly anti-racist activism carries with it the baggage of the cultural racism I am describing. Fully believing in one's own cultural superiority, the resolution of racial injustice lies in granting the oppressed races equal access to its fruits. The Victorian doctrine of the White Man's Burden lurks within the zealous campaign to "develop," to "modernize," to bring the benefits of technology to all the world, to remake their medical, educational, agricultural, economic, and political systems in the image of the West. We must remember that some of the most heinous acts of racial oppression were done in the name of uplifting the savages, Christianizing the heathens. For example, the abduction of two or three generations of Native Americans and their placement into boarding schools that purposely expunged their language and culture was infused with high-minded ideals. The idea was to bring them into the "melting pot" of America, to make them like us, to supersede a backward, superstitious, inferior culture with a modern, superior one.

We sound an echo of that attitude today when we make anti-racism too much about how people of color are underrepresented in (fill in the blank: the 1 percent of CEOs, doctors, professors

. . .) or overrepresented among the ranks of the poor or incarcerated. While these disparities come from real racism, current and especially historical, focusing on them alone risks overlooking deeper systemic injustice. It would not be very disruptive to the status quo to merely insert people of different skin color into its existing roles and relations. Those roles and relations themselves draw from the hegemonic cultural matrix we call white. So yes, if we take that matrix for granted as unchangeable, then racial justice is indeed a matter of representation. But is that breaking the monopoly of whiteness, or is that to become white themselves? This is what the Nigerian (yes, again, *that* Nigeria) intellectual, poet, and author Bayo Akomolafe rejects when he writes, "Needless to say, a steady undercurrent of self-loathing flowed through our lives—urging us to civilizational heights of whiteness. Urging us to wear three piece suits under a quizzical sun. Urging us to demonize our own traditions so that we could catch up with you."[11]

It is quite understandable that in a situation where one culture has vanquished another, that the vanquished should wish to join the victors. Traditionally, conservatives have said, "Too bad, we won and you lost," while liberals have said, "Oh, we must be nice and make a place for the less fortunate." Neither questions the desirability of the victory itself that spreads modern medicine and education, politics and science, money and markets, to all the world.

It might also look like here is a white person telling everyone else that they shouldn't want what I have, when all the world actually does want modern medicine, modern schooling, and economic development. They themselves say they want it—case closed. One must question, though, the context of this wanting. If I may quote myself, here is a passage from *The Ascent of Humanity* about how to destroy a culture and make it want to be like ours:

> Disrupt its networks of reciprocity by introducing consumer items from the outside. Erode its

self-esteem with glamorous images of the West. Demean its mythologies through missionary work and scientific education. Dismantle its traditional ways of transmitting local knowledge by introducing schooling with outside curricula. Destroy its language by providing that schooling in English or another national or world language. Truncate its ties to the land by importing cheap food to make local agriculture uneconomic. Then you will have created a people hungry for the right sneaker.[12]

As you can see, to argue, "They want their Nikes (that is, modern lifestyles) and it is racist of you to tell them they can't have it," leaves the whole process of colonization unexamined.

Please don't take this as an argument to do nothing about racially unequal access to medicine, food, power, and money. To the contrary, it is about meeting those needs outside the hegemonic white model. And do not take it as a criticism of those in oppressed groups who have striven to succeed in the white world. Theirs is a natural response to circumstances. What I am saying is that racial healing (and reparation) is much bigger than inclusion in the white-constructed and whitewashed world.

"Inclusivity" is a byword of the anti-racism movement, but it would be no victory for humanity if black people alongside white occupied the helm of the world-destroying humanity-exploiting machine. Too often, "inclusion" has meant erasure; it has meant acquiescence to the final, global victory of white culture. A true undoing of racism would not be to magnanimously "include" the formerly marginalized in the dominating culture, but rather to end the patterns of domination altogether. Many white people intuit this, which is why they yearn for inclusion themselves in cultures outside their own. While sometimes diverted onto cultural appropriation, the yearning also comes from a growing humility that recognizes maybe our culture isn't the best after all.

A similar point applies to another byword of race discourse, "privilege." The privilege discourse says, "White people, you have a seat at the banquet table, and others do not. Furthermore, you are directly benefiting from the deprivation of others." True as far as it goes, this narrative leaves out whether the banquet is really worth having. Blindly holding it to be a consummate feast, we assume that justice, equity, and advancement means to make room for everyone at our table, with its menu of modern medicine, free markets, mass schooling, and neoliberal democracy.

Hot Dogs and Cheese Fries

I think the situation is more as follows: The banquet is an orgy of gluttony, and the main dishes are hot dogs, cheese fries, and soda pop. The oppressed races and classes, in this system, receive but scraps from the banquet table—the same menu, but less of it. They receive an inferior version of liberal education, modern medicine, political freedom, and the rest of modern life. With due apologies to fans of hot dogs and cheese fries, it is no real solution to extend the orgy of gluttony to one and all. That would only make sense if hot dogs and cheese fries are all that there were. In truth, the situation is that all the best dishes have been purged from the menu. Justice is not to include everyone else in the banquet of whiteness. It is to stop imposing its menu on everyone else, and respectfully sample and share each other's dishes to create a diversity of coevolving banquets.

If hot dogs and cheese fries are all that is available, it is better to have them than to starve. Absent wealth equality, it is better to be rich than to be poor. Absent a system of communal land ownership and vernacular architecture, it is better to afford to buy a house than to be homeless. Absent community-based ways to regulate social behavior, it is better to have the police on your side. Absent strong traditions of folk medicine, it is better to have health insurance than to be locked out of the only health care available. Absent robust local food systems, it is better to be able to shop at Whole Foods than at a convenience store. Absent a robust gift culture, it is better to have money than to have none. In current circumstances, one is better off privileged than not; however, the privilege discourse implicitly elevates its own values. It posits the life of the wealthy suburbanite with full medical insurance, well-funded school, secure investment portfolio, friendly police force, well-equipped modern hospital, and easily accessible Whole Foods as the good life, if only it could be available to all, if only room could be made for others to sit at the banquet of whiteness.

Such a life, if expanded to all, is ecologically unsustainable, but the problem is deeper than that. It is also socially impossible to expand it to all, since the wealth of some rests necessarily on the poverty of others. Actually the problem is deeper than that, too. The banquet of whiteness is actually destitute of any real nourishment, as demonstrated by relentlessly rising rates of depression, suicide, mental illness, addiction, and divorce among those with the very best seats at the feast as well as those scrambling under the table for discarded bits of hot dog roll. Is this really the vision of the good life we would bring to one and all?

If you want to find the world's happiest people, don't look in Beverly Hills or the Hamptons. Look instead among the Hadza or the Q'ero, or go to a village in Ghana or Bhutan. It is not the West that has most highly developed the art of being human.

As for happiness, so also for health. What we might call "white medicine" has recorded miraculous successes, especially in emergency medicine. Overall, though, it is debatable whether our society is healthier than traditional societies. It is not only mental and social illnesses that are on the rise; chronic physical ailments are on the rise as well, for which modern medicine can sometimes palliate symptoms but offers little in the way of cure. Autoimmune diseases, allergies, metabolic disorders, and especially childhood chronic conditions run at unprecedented levels, increasing in each society in tandem with its modernization. In

1960, incidence of childhood chronic disease in the US was 1.8 percent; today it is over 50 percent.[13]

The association of modernity with declining health was observed in the early twentieth century by Weston A. Price, a dentist who traveled to remote parts of the world to document the health of people untouched by modern diets. From the Outer Hebrides to Polynesia, from Inuit villages to Maasai encampments, he compiled 15,000 photographs and innumerable descriptions of the magnificent health normal to those places: spacious palates with all thirty-two teeth, little tooth decay, no heart disease, easy childbirth, no chronic disease, and so forth. It was only with the introduction of modern foods and lifestyles that the maladies of modernity—which we take to be normal—became common. Once white diets and living patterns took hold, white medicine was also needed to handle the consequences. (Again, "white"— the cultures under assault were of every skin color.)

With the food and habits of the colonizers came the diseases of the colonizer. With the religion and worldview of the colonizer came its medical practices. If our own "modernity" is the inevitable destiny of the world, then so are the diseases of modernity, social or physical. Progress for the "underdeveloped" then means to bring them the medicine, education, and political systems developed to cope with those diseases.

That also means that to embrace TCM or African traditional medicine must go along with broader changes in thinking and living. Neither works very well as an add-on to an otherwise fully conventional life. That is why they are often a point of departure from a conventional life.

Given the menu most people have in hand, given the realities of modern life, palliative care to manage a disease is a lot better than what the poor and uninsured often receive, which is no care at all. Within its horizons, the privilege discourse is irrefutable. It takes for granted, however, many of the values and assumptions of the very world it is trying to overthrow.

What Is Real?

One way that well-meaning anti-racism activists try to grapple with the aforementioned ontological imperialism is to celebrate nonrational, experiential "other ways of knowing," contradistinguishing them from linear, rational, evidentiary white science. This attempt unfortunately smuggles in the same cultural superiority complex I've described. It is not that TCM or the belief systems underlying exorcism are illogical or ignorant of evidence. They merely issue from a different set of postulates, a different theory of change, and a different metaphysics. And they emphasize pattern logic over linear logic, synthetic thinking over analytic thinking, and teleology over reductionism.

Immersed in non-Western, nonscientific, nonwhite mythologies, one soon encounters evidence that makes them real. Modern thinking holds that there is reality, and then there are beliefs about reality. In so thinking, it stands at odds with other cultures in which the relationship between belief and reality, between subject and object, between name and thing was mysterious. Enter a worldview, utter its names, perform its rituals, and its denizens will come to greet you. Enter deeply the world of an actual voodoo priestess or Andean shaman or Taoist priest, and you will experience things that are impossible in the standard scientific worldview.

I once heard a story about the great anthropologist of religious Taoism, Kristofer Schipper, who served a long apprenticeship under Taoist priests in Taiwan. In the dead of night a knock at his door roused him from bed. Opening the door, he saw three animated corpses staring at him. "You have the wrong house!" he barked, slammed the door, and went back to bed. Relating the story to my friend, he said, "When you enter the world of folk Taoism, sometimes the undead pay you a visit." In that mythology, they are real.

What is real in our own (mainstream) mythology? Viruses, for one thing. (Note that our religion—science—bears its own heretics who don't believe that SARS-CoV-2 causes Covid-19, and they are treated, indeed, as exactly that: heretics.) Accordingly, we enact a set of rituals to ward off the evil spirit we call a virus. We don that most primal of ritual gear, a mask. We keep our distance from the unclean for fear the spirit will jump from them to us. We go through sanctification procedures like hand washing and disinfectant booths. Those seriously afflicted go to special temples (hospitals) where highly trained acolytes in ceremonial garb apply various magical potions, tablets, and ritual devices. However real and sensible these procedures are to us, that is how real and sensible the beliefs and practices of another culture are to them. We are tempted to privilege our own practices by saying they aren't rituals, that they are based on real cause and effect, that they are verifiable through the Scientific Method, not realizing that we might be inhabiting a self-reifying mythology.

Our present historical moment is one of transition in our mythology, in the basic narratives by which we know self and world. Having corroded the other cultures of the world, it now dissolves itself. The ingredients of the innumerable feasts of world cultures are strewn about the kitchen. To assemble them into something more sumptuous than ever before, we must first give up the idea that our dishes were the best. A new mythology is beckoning. For it to become real, we must develop the courage to release the old one, even though it once seemed like absolute reality itself. Fortunately, courage has an ally—reality has been falling apart for a while now. There is no doubt that economic reality and political reality have shifted. But the process of dissolution won't stop there.

Science itself is changing as long-held truisms collapse. For instance, for my entire life the scientific-political establishment derided the notion of extraterrestrial visitors to Earth, explaining away, with full weight of scientific authority, UFOs as just so many weather balloons, swamp gases, illusions, and hoaxes. Now even the *New York Times* and the US Navy admit to numerous accounts from trained observers of aerial phenomena far beyond the capabilities of current technology. Even science's basic metaphysical assumptions are wavering. Foremost among them are observer independence and the isolability of variables. Meditate on quantum nonlocality and the measurement paradox, or on nonlinear emergence and order out of chaos, or dig down into topics like the placebo effect, water memory, psi phenomena, the Bengston Method, and so on, and science, including medical science, looks more and more like the knowledge systems it has long demeaned. Rather than bringing other traditions to our banquet table, the future might have us leave the table to be hosted at others.

What applies to science and medicine extends into the rest of life. As our political systems putrefy, will we continue to try to impose them on the rest of the world? As our chemical- and machine-intensive agricultural system founders, do we continue to push it on Africa? Instead, we might acknowledge the crying need for all that modern culture has banished from our lives, let go of the superiority complex, and adopt the humility necessary to relearn folk medicine, local food systems, gift economies, experiential education, ways of ceremony and prayer, and the mindset and perceptions necessary to live in harmony with each other and the Earth.

To be sure, knowledge of these ways is not held exclusively by communities of color, but the dominant culture we are calling "white" has long suppressed or ignored it. Thankfully, it still remains in what Orland Bishop calls "cultures of memory": indigenous, traditional, and marginalized cultures, as well as hidden lineages within the dominant culture. Maybe Western civilization did not conquer the world after all. The appearance of conquest is temporary. The apparently vanquished cultures are still here, awaiting the exhaustion of our own. Some survive in remote places, relatively intact. Others persist in cultures like India and China that are too massive to be fully Westernized, and among minorities who have resisted full assimilation (expressed in practices like voodoo). Some are wrapped up within the main culture itself, imprinted onto its wisdom lineages, customs, super-stitions, underclasses, and countercultures. Even peoples who seem to have been totally extinguished bestowed seeds upon the future, suffusing the land with wisdom that may yet be recovered, ancient seeds awaiting the thousand-year flood. These cultures of memory provide the ingredients and the cookbooks from which humanity, collectively, might prepare a true feast.

Life of the Festival

JUNE 2021

Nearly ten months passed between the publication of "The Banquet of Whiteness" and this one, originally titled "The Death of the Festival," and I didn't publish any essays of any kind from February to June 2021. The reason was a profound psychic paralysis. I wrestled with despair, doubt, and fear, falling sometimes into fugues of despondency in which I could barely get out of bed. It wasn't depression. It was a soul-level doubt of everything I believed about myself and the world. Not only did I doubt my opinions; at times I doubted even my direct experiences.

In April 2021 I gave a live event in Colorado entitled "How to Stay Sane in Crazy Times." The kernel of the two-day affair was the following passage that I composed the morning before:

> *What makes you crazy is to be an agent of your own gaslighting. It starts with outward conformity, when you say and do things that contradict your truth. You might have good reasons to uphold the pretense: to avoid shaming and ostracism, to be accepted, to keep your job. But unless you can hold a place of truth within you that*

is inviolate, the show soon becomes real. You forget the boundary between true and false, and the bandits breach the walls. They run amok as you retreat to the inner sanctuary, the seat of the soul. Finally they usurp that too, and you become a fugitive in your own castle. That is what I mean by insanity.

The response of the participants was overwhelming. My reminder that they were not crazy (for doubting the whole Covid drama of masks, lockdowns, vaccines, contact tracing ... the upending of life in the name of safety) was like water in the desert, and the participants' reception of it poured that water back into my parched soul. The subtext of "You're not crazy" was "I'm not crazy, right?" Sanity, I realized, is a group project.

It was at that moment that I began to drop the shackles of fear and doubt and, after ten months, name what I saw happening in the world. I spent two months writing this essay, which grew to well over 10,000 words. I realized I needed to cut it up. This "Life of the Festival" part lays the conceptual groundwork of the five-part series, which I call the Girard series. It doesn't directly confront the prevailing Covid narrative, partly because I wanted it to be accessible to those who would discard it if it were more direct, and partly because my courage was still ripening. It was still safer to be philosophical about things and avoid statements that would invite attack. But I knew what was coming. I'd taken the first step down a slippery slope.

The theme of festival has taken on a new relevance as of early 2022 with the truckers' convoy and protests. The truckers who converged on Ottawa to protest vaccine mandates and Covid restrictions instigated a festival in the classic anthropological sense of suspending ordinary social conventions, as public space is devoted to nonordinary uses. The protests had both a festive aspect—with their bouncy castles, music, and creative artistic displays—and a ceremonial aspect, as they performed the rituals of political theater.

Predictably, the authorities reacted with horror and alarm. Their reaction was out of proportion to the political demands of the protest. Why not just negotiate? Because something much bigger was at stake. The very idea of Festival, erupting outside the boundaries of the normal social order, is terrifying to fascistic authorities whose goal is the totalization of the social order. That is why they are called totalitarians.

> We live a double life, civilized in scientific and technical matters, wild and primitive in the things of the soul. That we are no longer conscious of being primitive, makes our tamed kind of wildness all the more dangerous.
>
> —HANS VON HENTIG

The natural order is unraveling. Plagues, floods, droughts, political unrest, riots, and economic crises strike one upon the next, before society has recovered from the last. Cracks spread in the shell of normality that encloses human life. Societies have faced such circumstances repeatedly throughout history, just as we face them today.

We would like to think we are responding more rationally and more effectively than our unscientific forebears; instead, we enact age-old social dramas and superstitions dressed in the garb of modern mythology. No wonder, because the most serious crisis we face is not new.

None of the problems facing humanity today are technically difficult to solve. Holistic farming methods could heal soil and water, sequester carbon, increase biodiversity, and actually increase yields to swiftly solve various ecological and humanitarian crises. Simply declaring a moratorium on fishing in half the world's oceans would heal them, too. Systemic use of natural and alternative healing modalities could vastly reduce Covid mortality, and reverse the (objectively more serious) plagues of autoimmunity, allergies, and addiction. New economic arrangements could easily eradicate poverty. However, what all of these easy solutions have in common is that they require agreement among human beings. There is almost no limit to what a unified, coherent society can achieve. That is why the overarching crisis of our time—more serious than ecological collapse, more serious than economic collapse, more serious than the pandemic—is the polarization and fragmentation of civil society. With coherency, anything is possible. Without it, nothing is.

The late philosopher René Girard believed that this has always been true: Since prehistoric times, the greatest threat to society has been a breakdown in cohesion. Theologian S. Mark Heim elegantly lays out Girard's thesis: "Particularly in its infancy, social life is a fragile shoot, fatally subject to plagues of rivalry and vengeance. In the absence of law or government, escalating cycles of retaliation are the original social disease. Without finding a way to treat it, human society can hardly begin."[1]

The historical remedy is not very inspiring. Heim continues:

> The means to break this vicious cycle appear as if miraculously. At some point, when feud threatens to dissolve a community, spontaneous and irratio-nal mob violence erupts against some distinctive person or minority in the group. They are accused of the worst crimes the group can imagine, crimes that by their very enormity might have caused the terrible plight the community now experiences. They are lynched.
>
> The sad good in this bad thing is that it actually works. In the train of the murder, communities find

that this sudden war of all against one has delivered them from the war of each against all. The sacrifice of one person as a scapegoat discharges the pending acts of retribution. It "clears the air." The sudden peace confirms the desperate charges that the victim had been behind the crisis to begin with. If the scapegoat's death is the solution, the scapegoat must have been the cause. The death has such reconciling effect, that it seems the victim must possess supernatural power. So the victim becomes a criminal, a god, or both, memorialized in myth.[2]

The buildup of reciprocal violence and anarchy that precedes this resolution was described by Girard in his masterwork, *Violence and the Sacred*, as a "sacrificial crisis." Divisions rend society, violence and vengeance escalate, people ignore the usual restraints and morals, and the social order dissolves into chaos. This culminates in a transition from reciprocal violence to unanimous violence: The mob selects a victim (or class of victims) for slaughter and in that act of universal agreement, restores social order.

The Age of Reason has not uprooted this deep pattern of redemptive violence. Reason but serves to rationalize it; industry takes it to industrial scale, and high technology threatens to lift it to new heights. As society has grown more complex, so too have the variations on the theme of redemptive violence. Yet the pattern can be broken. The first step to doing that is to see it for what it is.

In order that full-blown sacrificial crises need not repeat, an institution arose that is nearly universal across human societies: the festival. Girard draws extensively from ethnography, myth, and literature to make the case that festivals originated as ritual reenactments of the breakdown of order and its subsequent restoration through violent unanimity.

A true festival is not a tame affair. It is a suspension of normal rules, mores, structures, and social distinctions. Girard explains:

> Such violations [of legal, social, and sexual norms] must be viewed in their broadest context: that of the overall elimination of differences. Family and social hierarchies are temporarily suppressed or inverted; children no longer respect their parents, servants their masters, vassals their lords. This motif is reflected in the esthetics of the holiday—the display of clashing colors, the parading of transvestite figures, the slapstick antics of piebald "fools." For the duration of the festival unnatural acts and outrageous behavior are permitted, even encouraged.
>
> As one might expect, this destruction of differences is often accompanied by violence and strife. Subordinates hurl insults at their superiors; various social factions exchange gibes and abuse. Disputes rage in the midst of disorder. In many instances the motif of rivalry makes its appearance in the guise of a contest, game, or sporting event that has assumed a quasi-ritualistic cast. Work is suspended, and the celebrants give themselves over to drunken revelry and the consumption of all the food amassed over the course of many months.[3]

Festivals of this kind serve to cement social coherence and remind society of the catastrophe that lays in wait should that coherence falter. Faint vestiges of them remain today, for example in football hooliganism, street carnivals, music festivals, and the Halloween phrase "trick or treat." The "trick" is a relic of the temporary upending of the established social order. Druidic scholar Philip Carr-Gomm describes Samhuinn, the Celtic precursor to Halloween, like this:

Samhuinn, from 31 October to 2 November was a time of no-time. Celtic society, like all early societies, was highly structured and organised, everyone knew their place. But to allow that order to be psychologically comfortable, the Celts knew that there had to be a time when order and structure were abolished, when chaos could reign. And Samhuinn was such a time. Time was abolished for the three days of this festival and people did crazy things, men dressed as women and women as men. Farmers' gates were unhinged and left in ditches, peoples' horses were moved to different fields . . .[4]

In modern, "developed" societies today, neither Halloween nor any other holiday or culturally sanctioned event permits this level of anarchy. Our holidays have been fully tamed. This does not bode well. Girard writes:

The joyous, peaceful facade of the deritualized festival, stripped of any reference to a surrogate victim and its unifying powers, rests on the framework of a sacrificial crisis attended by reciprocal violence. That is why genuine artists can still sense that tragedy lurks somewhere behind the bland festivals, the tawdry utopianism of the "leisure society." The more trivial, vulgar, and banal holidays become, the more acutely one senses the approach of something uncanny and terrifying.[5]

That last sentence strikes a chord of foreboding. For decades I've looked at the degenerating festivals of my culture with an alarm I couldn't quite place. As All Hallows' Eve devolved into a minutely supervised children's game from 6 to 8 pm, as the Rites of Resurrection devolved into the Easter Bunny and jellybeans, and Yule into an orgy of consumption, I perceived that we were stifling ourselves in a box of mundanity, a totalizing domesticity that strove to maintain a narrowing order by shutting out wildness completely. The result, I thought, could only be an explosion.

It is not just that festivals are necessary to blow off steam. They are necessary to remind us of the artificiality and frailty of the human ordering of the world, lest we go insane within it.

Mass insanity comes from the denial of what everyone knows is true. Every human being knows, if only unconsciously, that we are not the roles and personae we occupy in the cultural drama of life. We know the rules of society are arbitrary, set up so that the show can be played out to its conclusion. It is not insane to enter this show, to strut and fret one's hour upon the stage. Like an actor in a movie, we can devotedly play our roles in life. But when the actor forgets he is acting and loses himself so fully in his role that he cannot get out of it, mistaking the movie for reality, that's psychosis. Without respite from the conventions of the social order and without respite from our roles within it, we go crazy, as well.

We should not be surprised that Western societies are showing signs of mass psychosis. The vestigial festivals that remain today—the aforementioned holidays, along with cruise ships and parties and bars—are contained within the spectacle and do not stand outside it. As for Burning Man and the transformational music and art festivals, these have exercised some of the festival's authentic function—until recently, when their exile to online platforms stripped them of any transcendental possibility. Much as the organizers are doing their best to keep the idea of the festival alive, online festivals risk becoming just another show for consumption. One clicks into them, sits back, and watches. In-person festivals are different. They start with a journey, then one must undergo an ordeal (waiting in line for hours). Finally you get to the entrance temple (the registration booth), where a small divination ritual (checking the list) is performed to determine your fitness to attend (by having made the appropriate sacrifice—a payment—beforehand). Thereupon, the priest or priestess in the booth confers upon the celebrant a special talisman to wear around the wrist at all times. After all this, the subconscious mind understands one has entered a separate realm, where indeed, to a degree at least, normal distinctions, relations, and rules do not apply. Online events of any kind rest safely in the home. Whatever the content, the body recognizes it as a show.

More generally, locked in, locked down, and locked out, the population's confinement within the highly controlled environment of the internet is driving them crazy. By "controlled" I do not here refer to censorship, but rather to the physical experience of being seated watching depictions of the real, absent any tactile or kinetic dimension. Online, there is no such thing as a risk. Okay, sure, someone can hurt your feelings, ruin your reputation, or steal your credit card number, but all these operate within the cultural drama. They are not of the same order as crossing a stream on slippery rocks, or walking in the heat, or hammering in a nail. Because conventional reality is artificial, the human being needs regular connection to a reality that is nonconventional in order to remain sane. That hunger for unprogrammed, wild, real experiences—real food for the soul—intensifies beneath the modern diet of canned holidays, online adventures, classroom exercises, safe leisure activities, and consumer choices.

Absent authentic festivals, the pent-up need erupts in spontaneous quasi-festivals that follow the Girardian pattern. One name for such a festival is a riot. In a riot, as in an authentic festival, prevailing norms of conduct are upended. Boundaries and taboos around private property, trespassing, use of streets and public spaces, and the like dissolve for the duration of the "festival." This enactment of social disintegration culminates either in genuine mob violence or some cathartic pseudo-violence (which can easily spill over into the real thing). An example is toppling statues, an outright ritual substituting symbolic action for real action even in the name of "taking action." Yes, I understand its rationale (dismantling narratives that involve symbols of oppression, white supremacy, and so forth), but its main function is as a unifying act of symbolic violence. However, this cathartic release of social tensions does little to change the deep conditions that give rise to those tensions in the first place. Thus it helps to maintain them.

I became aware of the festive dimension to riots while teaching at a university in the early 2000s. Some of my students participated in a riot following a home-team basketball victory. It started as a celebration, but soon they were smashing windows, stealing street signs, removing farmers' gates from their hinges, and otherwise violating the social order. These violations also took on a creative dimension reminiscent of street carnivals. One student recounted making a gigantic "the finger" out of foam and parading it around town. "It was the most fun I've had my whole life," he said. More than any contained, neutered holiday, this was an authentic festival seeking to be born. And it wasn't safe. People were accidentally injured. A real festival is serious business. Normal laws and customs, morals and conventions, do not govern it. A festival may evolve its own traditions, but these originate organically, not imposed by authorities of the normal, conventional order; else, it is not a real festival. A real festival is essentially a repeated, ritualized riot that has evolved its own pattern language.

The more locked down, policed, and regulated a society, the less tolerance there is for anything outside its order. Eventually but one microfestival remains—the joke. To not take things so seriously is to stand outside its reality; it is to affirm for a moment that this isn't as real as we are making it, that there is something outside this. There is truth in a joke, the same truth that is in a festival. It is a respite from the total enclosure of conventional reality. That is why totalitarian movements are so hostile to humor, with the sole exception of the kind that degrades and mocks their opponents. (Mocking humor, such as racist humor, is in fact an instrument of dehumanization in preparation for scapegoating.) In Soviet Russia one could be sent to the Gulag for telling the wrong joke; in that country, it was also jokes that kept people sane. Humor can be deeply subversive—not only by making authorities seem ridiculous, but by making light of the reality they attempt to impose.

Because it undermines conventional reality, humor is also a primal peace offering. It says, "Let's not take our opposition so seriously." That is not to say we should joke all the time, using humor to deflect intimacy and distract from the roles we have agreed to play in the drama of the human social experience, any more than life should be an endless festival. But because humor acts as a kind of microfestival to tether us to a transcendent reality, a society of good humor is likely to be a healthy society that needn't veer into sacrificial violence. And a society that attempts to confine its jokes within politically correct bounds faces the same "uncanny and terrifying" prospects as a society that has tamed its festivals. Humorlessness is a sign that a sacrificial crisis is on its way.

The loss of sanity that results from confinement in unreality is itself a Girardian sacrificial crisis, the essential feature of which is internecine violence. One might think that with little but hurt feelings at stake, online interactions would be less fraught with conflict than in-person interactions. But of course it is the reverse. One way to understand it is that absent a transcendental perspective outside the orderly, conventional realm of "life," trivial things loom large and we start taking life much too seriously. This is not to deny the substance of our disagreements, but do we really need to go to war over them? Is the other side whose shortcomings we blame for our problems really so awful? As Girard observes, "The same creatures who are at each others' throats during the course of a sacrificial crisis are fully capable of coexisting, before and after the crisis, in the relative harmony of a ritualistic order."[6]

Surveying the social media landscape, it is clear that we are indeed at each others' throats, and there is no guarantee that that will remain a mere figure of speech as something uncanny and terrifying approaches.

Fascism and the Antifestival

JUNE 2021

This essay broaches the core topic of the Girard series: fascism. It doesn't yet issue an explicit warning that we are quickly heading toward fascism. I was still gathering my courage and my clarity, still making sure that I was seeing what I was seeing. It is so much easier not to see. I think I was also being strategic, insinuating the idea that society had taken a fascistic turn without directly talking about medical totalitarianism and the biosecurity state.

The other main point of this piece is simply to establish that something else is happening besides a medical emergency. The medical emergency—if an emergency it is—is a vehicle for the expression of primal social forces. One of those archetypal forces is religious hysteria, a close cousin of the mob dynamics I describe in this essay's sequel, "Mob Morality and the Unvaxxed."

Today, the Western world and particularly the United States appears to be in the midst of a classic Girardian sacrificial crisis. Once-reliable social institutions crumble. The public loses trust in its authorities: political, financial, legal, and medical. The new generation is poorer and sicker than the last. Few of any political persuasion believe that society is working or that we are on the right track. Reason, markets, and technology have failed to redeem their utopian promise. The gods have failed us, and we glimpse monsters emerging from their shadows: ecological collapse, nuclear Armageddon, the poisoning of our bodies, minds, and world. Simmering differences and rivalries, once subsumed under a general civic consensus, take on a new intensity as each side grows more militant. As confidence wanes in the state's capacity to hold evil at bay, latent ritualistic instincts come back to life.

Philosopher René Girard argued that these ritualistic instincts derive from social upheavals in which runaway cycles of vengeance—the original social disease—were converted into unifying violence against scapegoated victims. Rituals, religions, festivals, and political institutions evolved to prevent similar outbreaks from recurring.

One such ritual pattern that Girard identifies is the "antifestival," in which "the rites of sacrificial expulsion are not preceded by a period of frenzied anarchy, but by an extreme austerity and an increased rigor in the observance of all interdicts."[1] In modern times the antifestival takes an extended institutional form in totalitarianism. Both Soviet Communism and Nazi fascism had a strong puritanical streak, as both were hostile to anything outside their own order. Fascism is essentially an extended antifestival, and it arises, as does the antifestival, in response to looming social breakdown, real or imagined. In many societies, the priestly caste takes every opportunity to impose rigorous interdicts, taboos, and rituals, which all serve to increase their own power. The best opportunity is a crisis that can be attributed to people's sinful ways. A crisis like an earthquake, a flood, or . . . a plague.

We seem today to be partially emerging from an extended series of antifestivals, otherwise known as "lockdowns." They have accompanied totalitarian tendencies and a quasi-fascistic hostility to true festivals or indeed to anything resembling public fun. Moreover, many of our public health measures bear a distinct ritualistic cast, and share with both fascism and with numerous archaic antifestivals an obsession with "pollution." Consider the following passage from the early twentieth-century anthropologist James Frazer, entitled "The Collapse of the Nredom Tribe: A Case of Religious Hysteria":

> Jenkins' chronicle begins at a moment when the Nredom "tribe" (actually a numerous and highly organized society) was already showing signs of social, political, and ecological decline. For years its priests had been warning of evil spirits on the verge of attacking the people. Finally on the third year of Jenkins' ethnographic residency, some members of the tribe began to take ill. An evil spirit was afoot! As the priests explained it, the spirit could possess anyone who did not abide by various new taboos and perform necessary rituals. Once possessed by the spirit, a person became unclean, at risk of transmitting it to anyone they associated with. No one could see the spirit without special ceremonial instruments such as the priests possessed, but they made drawings of it to show the populace.
>
> A ritual was devised to determine whether any given person was possessed by the spirit. A specially consecrated wand was moistened with the bodily fluids of the person suspected of possession, and then sent to a special hut where priests would subject the stick to further divinatory rituals designed to force the evil spirit to reveal itself. Thereupon, agents of the priests would notify the unfortunate tribesperson of his or her possession. Anyone so adjudged of

possession had to remain in strict separation from the rest of the tribe for a fortnight.

Some of the taboos and rituals that the unfortunate superstitious natives adopted were quite bizarre. For example, the priests had marks placed a fathom-length apart in all public places, stating that if everyone stood no closer to each other than the marks indicated, that they would enjoy magical protection. They also demanded that everyone who might come into proximity to the unclean perform frequent ritual ablutions and other forms of bodily purification, and wear various forms of ceremonial headgear to frighten off the spirit. All public gatherings were prohibited, and even normal functions of life severely curtailed. No activity was permitted except with the priests' explicit sanction.

As you can imagine, this regime generated intense social stress, hardship, and some degree of opposition. Soon the priests were busy stamping out various heresies. Some heretics claimed that the rituals to stop transmission of the evil spirit wouldn't work, or that the spirit was not so dangerous. Some heretics doubted in the very existence of the evil spirit, saying the heightened levels of sickness were due to some other cause. Others loudly proclaimed that the evil spirit had been loosed upon the populace by the priests themselves. Social tensions mounted as the priests tried to silence the heretics and arouse the populace against them.

Most people in the tribe trusted the priests, but many apparently harbored doubts too, because adherence to the rituals was inconsistent. Knowing that public rejection of the strict regime of taboos and rituals was inevitable, the priests announced they were developing a new sacrament, a magic potion that would protect the recipient forever from possession. Administered by a deputized priest via a slightly painful ritual of skin piercing, the potion sanctified all those who received it. These sanctified brethren could engage in normal life again, although they still had to abide by certain of the new rituals and taboos. Those refusing the potion remained unclean and were subject to all kinds of penalties, shaming, and ostracism.

Unfortunately, the new potion proved less effective than the priests originally promised. According to the priests, other ghosts and spirits were lying in wait, against whom new rituals and taboos must be applied and new potions administered. The power given unto the priests in this time of crisis would need to be permanent. And, they hinted darkly, this plague of evil was a kind of punishment for the tribe's sinful ways, particularly the sins of the heretics. Heresy must be stamped out! The unclean must be sanctified! Soon religious pogroms swept the land, followed by counter-pogroms against the priests themselves. And Nredom society collapsed.

Okay, I confess. I made up this passage. The priests are the scientists. The wand is the PCR test swab. The unclean are those who test positive for Covid-19. The potion is the vaccine. My point is not that Covid is nothing but a religious hysteria. My point is that, whatever else Covid is, *it is also a religious hysteria*; that this lens greatly illuminates our current condition and quite probably upcoming events. Our social responses to Covid bear so striking a resemblance to ritual practices and ideas (masks, potions, tabooed persons, sanctification, and so forth) that we have to ask how much of our public health policy is really scientific, and how much is religion in disguise. It might even lead to a deeper question: how and whether science differs from (other) religions. (Before you start protesting, "Ridiculous. What about objectivity? The Scientific Method? Peer review?" please read the section "In Science We Trust" of my book *Climate: A New Story*. The idea cannot be dismissed on trivial grounds.)

I hesitate to call anything "just a ritual," which is a dismissal that ignores the mysterious relationship between ritual and reality; however, the dubious efficacy of many of our public health practices invites the judgment that they are, indeed, "just rituals." I will not attempt here to make a case that masks, lockdowns, distancing, and so forth are dubious. Ultimately the argument comes down to whether our systems of knowledge production (science and journalism) are sound, and whether our medical and political authorities are trustworthy. To doubt public health orthodoxy is to answer no, they are not sound, they are not trustworthy. However, anyone who tries to make this case must, by necessity, source evidence from outside official institutions— evidence which, for the true believers, is illegitimate by definition.

One is unlikely to prove the priests wrong using information sanctioned by the priests. If you try, you are exposed as a heretic.

One contemporary term for a heretic is a "conspiracy theorist." The term belongs in quotes because it is one thing to claim our institutions are unsound, and quite another to claim that a conscious conspiracy makes them so. "Conspiracy theorist" has become one of the ways to dismiss and dehumanize dissidents to public health orthodoxy.

The swiftness with which deviants from Covid orthodoxy are consigned to subhuman categories is alarming. It is just what is needed to prepare them for their role as Girardian scapegoats. A perennial human reflex, in times of trouble, is to find or create heretics and outcasts. Today they are called "anti-maskers," "anti-vaxxers," "science deniers," "Q-adjacent," "conspiracy theorists," "covidiots," and "domestic extremists," subjects of a kind of virtual pogrom that humiliates, blames, and often digitally extinguishes its targets. And sometimes the consequences are more than digital.

Like modern fascists with their ideas of ethnic cleansing, and modern Communists with their party purges, ancient societies according to Girard were often obsessed with pollution. The original pollutant was violence, which once instigated could quickly spread out of control, much like an infection. To quote Girard, "If the sacrificial catharsis actually succeeds in preventing the unlimited propagation of violence, a sort of infection is in fact being checked. . . . The tendency of violence to hurl itself on a surrogate if deprived of its original object can surely be described as a contaminating process."[2] Thus it was that sacrificial victims were often quarantined from normal society, and that the violence of the sacrifice was strictly contained within ritual structures.

What totalitarian societies, traditional antifestivals, and Covid lockdowns have in common is a reflex of control. This reflex meets any failure of control with more of it. When herbicide-resistant weeds appear, the solution is a new herbicide. When immigrants cross the border, we build a wall. When a school shooter gets into a locked school building, we fortify it further. When germs develop resistance to antibiotics, we invent new and stronger ones. When masks fail to stop the spread of Covid, we wear two. When our taboos fail to keep evil at bay, we redouble them. The controlling mind foresees a paradise in which every action and every object is monitored, labeled, and controlled. There will be no room for any bad thing to exist. Nothing and no one will be out of place. Every action will be authorized. Everyone will be safe.

Those who attribute the controlling programs of Bill Gates and the technocratic elite to malice do not see the idealism behind the Technological Program. To the elites, their critics seem incomprehensible: deluded, ignorant enemies of progress itself, enemies of the betterment of humanity.

Unfortunately for them and for us, the paradise of total control is a mirage, receding all the more quickly the faster we approach it. The more tightly we impose order, the more chaos squeezes out through the cracks. Girard: "Violence too long held in check will overflow its bounds—and woe to those who happen to be nearby."[3] The same for other aspects of the wild: desire, anger, fear, eros. Extreme order creates its opposite.

A subtle parallel connects the dynamics of the sacrificial victim with other programs of control. Ultimately, both depend on a false reduction whose temporary appearance of success allows deeper problems to persist. The cause of immigration is not just immigrants; the cause of school shootings is not just shooters; the cause of disease is not just pathogens; the cause of climate change is not just greenhouse gases. These are but the terminal agents of a long process; they are the most conspicuous among a complex of causes; they are, like a scapegoat, convenient targets for the exercise of power. Having exercised it, we rest satisfied that something has been done.

Mob Morality and
the Unvaxxed

AUGUST 2021

After I published this essay, a dear friend wrote to me, "What were you thinking? Why did you stick your neck out?" In publishing this essay I took the irreversible step from suspect character to outright heretic. It resulted from a long process of clarifying what within me was genuine uncertainty, and what was cowardice masquerading as uncertainty. It was only when I felt pretty clear about the difference that I knew it was time to take the irreversible step this essay proved to be.

When I got that clarity, I had to act. I believed, and still believe, that without action the trajectory of the world toward a totalitarian dystopia will not change. Not of its own accord. Certainly, I personally could keep my head down and, when things get bad, flee to some freer part of the world, but what about my children? My grandchildren? If we don't take a stand here, then where? If we don't take a stand now, then when?

The fears that had held me in check proved to be well-founded. In an ironic demonstration of the essay's thesis, the mob converged on me and the denunciations, cancellations, and "unsubscribes" poured in. My former publisher, North Atlantic Books, used the home page of their website to denounce me as an anti-Semite and purveyor of disinformation, demanding that I apologize and donate all my book royalties to a charity of their choice (to make vaccines available to the underprivileged). People wrote to the hosts of programs I was on demanding that I be removed. Podcasters who had interviewed me were asked to "distance themselves." At this writing, four months later, people still forward me righteous messages from those who don't want to be on a platform with me because of my "anti-Semitic rhetoric."

It was also true that my fears were not well-founded. On the grand scale of the human drama, none of this was really so bad. I probably gained more subscribers than I lost. I learned which of my friends was willing to stand by me in a pinch, when associating with me might tarnish their own reputation. And a new wellspring of energy bubbled up within me, now that I was no longer keeping my truth in check.

One significant aspect of the vitriolic response to this essay was its absurdity. Really, anti-Semite? You can't find a much more Jewish name than Eisenstein. (In fact, I am only half-Jewish, but I'm proud of my Jewish heritage and deeply respectful of the wisdom the Jewish religion carries.) One concerned friend sent the essay to several rabbis, who were perplexed as to what about it was anti-Semitic. I addressed the issue in a short follow-up essay that I have not included in this book. Anyway, the charge is absurd, and that very absurdity is significant because it demonstrates a key feature of mob dynamics. As I say in the Girard essay series, it matters little whether the sacrificial victim is innocent or guilty. All that is necessary is that a dehumanizing mark be affixed to him, so that everyone can recognize who the target is. The alacrity of the mob to pile on demonstrated that, indeed, our society is just as prone as ancient sacrificial societies, and maybe just as prone as 1930s Europe, to eruptions of mob violence that can be co-opted by fascistic political powers.

While this book is named after my first Covid-era essay, "The Coronation," this essay, "Mob Morality and the Unvaxxed" is its lynchpin. Self-doubt afflicted me sporadically after I published it, and to this day I am uncertain about many aspects of the Covid phenomenon, but with this essay the die was cast. I knew what was mine to do.

> Propaganda must facilitate the displacement of aggression by specifying the targets for hatred.
> —JOSEPH GOEBBELS

We would like to think that modern societies like ours have outgrown barbaric customs like human sacrifice. Sure, we still engage in scapegoating and figuratively sacrifice people on the altar of public opinion, but we don't actually kill people in hopes of placating the gods and restoring order. Or do we?

Some scholars believe we do. Following the thought of the late philosopher René Girard, they argue that human sacrifice is still with us today in the form of capital punishment (and incarceration—a removal from society). Girard believed that human sacrifice arose in response to what he called a "sacrificial crisis." The original sacrificial crisis—the greatest threat to early societies—was escalating cycles of violence and retribution. The solution was to redirect the vengeance away from each other and, in violent unanimity, toward a scapegoat or class of scapegoats. Once established, this pattern was memorialized in myth and ritual, applied preemptively as human sacrifice, and carried out in response to any other crisis that threatened society.

In this view, capital punishment originated in human sacrifice and it *is* human sacrifice. It performs the same function: to forestall reciprocal violence through unanimous violence. It does so by monopolizing vengeance, truncating the cycle of retaliatory violence at the first iteration. *This works whether the subject of execution or incarceration is guilty of a crime or not.* Justice is a cover story for something more primal. Theologian Brian K. Smith writes:

> The subject of a modern execution might also be carrying multivalent significations. Among other things (i.e., racial and economic metonymic potentialities), such a figure might serve as the representative of all crime, of "disorder" and social "chaos," of the "breakdown of values," etc. Apart from any utilitarian deterrent effect capital punishment might have, it is one, rather drastic, response to a social problem—illegal and illicit violence.[1]

In other words, what we rationalize in the language of justice and deterrence is actually a blood ritual, in which a person, whether guilty or not, becomes a symbol. Ritual springs up irrepressibly around executions: the last meal, the "dead man walking" to the special execution chamber, the witnesses, the medical procedures, the presiding physician, the signed papers, the last rites, the covering of the head, the precise timetable, the final words, and the exacting attention to detail all mark off the execution as separate, special . . . sacred.

Something Must Be Done

In a lucidly argued paper, legal scholar Roberta Harding offers several examples from the Deep South during Jim Crow where judge, jury, and prosecutor well knew that the accused black man was innocent of the charge of raping a white woman.[2] However, because the white supremacist social order was threatened by consensual interracial intercourse, they executed the accused anyway; if they failed to do so promptly he was lynched. Partly this was to set an example and terrify the black population, but partly it was because *something must be done.*

By the same token, it mattered little that Afghan villagers or Iraqi politicians had no culpability for 9/11; nor did it matter that bombing them would have no practical effect on future terrorism (except to further inflame it). Obviously, the United States was using 9/11 as a pretext to accomplish larger geopolitical aims. Yet it worked as a pretext only because of broad public agreement that "something must be done." And, enacting the age-old pattern, we knew what to do: find some target of unifying violence that cannot effectively retaliate. I was dismayed in 2001 when, at a Quaker meeting, of all places, one of the Quakers said, "Of course, a forceful response of some kind is necessary." What, I wondered, does "forceful" mean? It means bombing someone. In other words, we must find someone upon whom to visit violence. He might also have mentioned addressing the imperialist causes of terrorism, but those were not the subject "of course." Nearly everyone instinctively took for granted the necessity of finding sacrificial victims. We were definitely going to bomb someone—the only question was whom.

The 9/11 attack exemplifies what Harding calls a *triggering incident*, which "resuscitates dissensions, rivalries, jealousies and quarrels within the community," leading to a sacrificial crisis. A recent such incident was the murder of George Floyd, in May 2020. The latent conflicts it exposed have been festering for so long that it takes little provocation for them to erupt into an active crisis. The response to Floyd's murder was a classic illustration of the calming power of violent unanimity, as was the conviction and sentencing of the police officer who killed him, Derek Chauvin, which temporarily quelled the racialized civil unrest that the killing sparked. Something was done—but only to quell the unrest, not to solve the complex, heavily ramified problem of police killings. It no more addressed the source of America's race problems than killing Osama bin Laden made America safe from terrorism.

Not just any victim will do as an object of human sacrifice. Victims must be, as Harding describes it, "in" the community but not "of" it.[3] That is why, during the Black Death, mobs roamed about murdering Jews for "poisoning the wells." The entire Jewish population of Basel was burned alive, a scene repeated throughout Western Europe. Yet this was not mainly the result of preexisting virulent hatred of Jews waiting for an excuse to erupt; it was that victims were needed to release social tension and hatred, an instrument of that release, coalesced opportunistically on the Jews. They qualified as victims because of their in-but-not-of status.

"Combatting hatred" is combatting a symptom.

Scapegoats needn't be guilty, but they must be marginal, outcasts, heretics, taboo-breakers, or infidels of one kind or another. If they are too alien, they will be unsuitable as transfer objects of in-group aggression. Neither can they be full members of society, lest cycles of vengeance ensue. If they are not already marginal, they must be made so. It was ritually important that Derek Chauvin be cast as a racist and white supremacist; then his removal from society could serve symbolically as the removal of racism itself.

Just to be clear here, I am not saying Derek Chauvin's conviction for George Floyd's murder was unjust. I am saying that justice was not the only thing carried out.

Representatives of Pollution

Aside from criminals, who today serves as the representative of Smith's "disorder," "social chaos," and "breakdown of values" that seem to be overtaking the world? For most of my life, external enemies and a story-of-the-nation served to unify society: Communism and the Soviet Union, Islamic terrorism, the mission to the moon, and the mythology of progress. Today the Soviet Union is long dead, terrorism has ceased to terrify, the moon is boring, and the mythology of progress is in terminal decline. Civil strife burns ever hotter, without the broad consensus necessary to transform it into unifying violence. For the Right, it is Antifa, Black Lives Matter protesters, critical race theory academics, and undocumented immigrants that represent social chaos and the breakdown of values. For the Left it is the Proud Boys, right-wing militias, white supremacists, QAnon, the Capitol rioters, and the burgeoning new category of "domestic extremists." And finally, defying left-right categorization is a promising new scapegoat class, the heretics of our time: the anti-vaxxers. As a readily identifiable subpopulation, they are ideal candidates for scapegoating.

It matters little whether any of these pose a real threat to society. As with the subjects of criminal justice, their guilt is irrelevant to the project of restoring order through blood sacrifice (or expulsion from the community by incarceration or, in more tepid but possibly prefigurative form, through "canceling"). All that is necessary is that the dehumanized class arouse the blind indignation and rage necessary to incite a paroxysm of unifying violence. More relevant to current times, this primal mob energy can be harnessed toward fascistic political ends. Totalitarians right and left invoke it directly when they speak of purges, ethnic cleansing, racial purity, and traitors in our midst.

Sacrificial subjects carry an association of pollution or contagion; their removal thus cleanses society. I know people in the alternative health field who are considered so unclean that if I so much as mention their names in a tweet or Facebook post, the post may be deleted. Deletion is a certainty if I link to an article or interview with them. The public's ready acceptance of such blatant censorship cannot be explained solely in terms of its believing the pretext of "controlling misinformation." Unconsciously, the public recognizes and conforms to the age-old program of investing a pariah subclass with the symbology of pollution.

This program is well underway toward the Covid-unvaxxed, who are being portrayed as walking cesspools of germs who might contaminate the sanctified brethren (the vaccinated). My wife perused a Facebook page today on acupuncture (which one would expect to be skeptical of mainstream medicine) where someone asked, "What is the word that comes to mind to describe unvaccinated people?" The responses were things like "filth," "assholes," and "death-eaters." This is precisely the dehumanization necessary to prepare a class of people for cleansing.

The science behind this portrayal is dubious. Contrary to the association of the unvaccinated with public danger, some experts contend that it is the vaccinated who are more likely to drive mutant variants through selection pressure. Just as antibiotics result in higher mutation rates and adaptive evolution in bacteria, leading to antibiotic resistance, so may vaccines push viruses to mutate. (Hence the prospect of endless "boosters" against endless new variants.) This phenomenon has been studied for decades.[4] The mutated variants evade the vaccine-induced antibodies, in contrast to the robust immunity that, according to some scientists, those who have already been sick with Covid have to all variants.[5]

It is not my purpose here, however, to present a scientific case. My point is that those in the scientific and medical community who dissent from the demonization of the unvaxxed contend not only with opposing scientific views but also with ancient, powerful psycho-social forces. They can debate the science all they want, but they are up against something much bigger. Rwandan scientists could just as well have debated the precepts of Hutu Power for all the good that would have done. Perhaps the Nazi example is more apposite here, since the Nazis did invoke science in their extermination campaigns. Then as now, science was a cloak for something more primal. The hurricane of sacrificial violence easily swept aside the minority of German scientists who contested the science of eugenics, and it wasn't because the dissidents were wrong.

We face a similar situation today. If the mainstream view on Covid vaccines is wrong, it will not be overthrown by science alone. The pro-vaccine camp has a powerful nonscientific ally in the collective id, expressed through various mechanisms of ostracism, shaming, and other social and economic pressure. It takes courage to defy a mob. Doctors and scientists who express anti-vaccine views risk losing funding, jobs, and licenses, just as ordinary citizens face censorship on social media. Even a nonpolemic essay like this one will likely be censored, especially if I stain it with the pollution of the heretics by linking blacklisted websites or articles by the "disinformation dozen" anti-vaxxers. Here, let's try it for fun. GreenMedInfo! Children's Health Defense! Mercola.com! Ah. That felt a little like shouting swear words in public. You'd better not visit these websites, lest you be tainted by their pollution (and your browsing history mark you as an infidel).

To prepare someone for removal as the repository of all that is evil, it helps to heap upon them every imaginable calumny. Thus we hear in mainstream publications that anti-vaxxers not only are killing people but are raging narcissists, white supremacists, vile spreaders of Russian disinformation, and tantamount to domestic terrorists.[6] These accusations are amplified by cherry-picking a few examples, choosing hysterical-looking photos of anti-vaxxers, and showcasing their most dubious arguments. If the authorities follow the playbook developed to counter other domestic "threats," we can also expect agents-provocateurs, entrapment schemes, government agents voicing violent positions to discredit the movement, and so forth—techniques developed in the infiltration of the civil rights, environmental, and antiglobalism movements.

Concerned friends have advised me to "distance myself" from members of the disinformation dozen whom I know, as if they carry some kind of contagion. Well, in a sense they do—the contagion of disrepute. It reminds me of Soviet times when mere association with a dissident could land one in the Gulag with them. It also reminds me of my school days, when it was social suicide to be friendly with the weird kid, whose weirdness would rub off on oneself. In grade school, this contagion was known as "cooties." (In my early teens *I* was the weird kid, and only very brave teenagers would be friendly to me while anyone was watching.) Clearly, the basic social dynamic pervades society at many levels. A deeply ingrained gut instinct recognizes the danger of membership in a pariah subclass. To defend the pariahs or to fail to show sufficient enthusiasm in attacking them marks one with suspicion; the result is self-censorship and discretion, contributing all the more to the illusion of unanimity.

Hijacking Morality

The same kind of positive reinforcement cycle is what generates a mob. All it takes is a few loud people to incite it by declaring someone or something a target. A portion of the crowd goes along enthusiastically. The rest keep silent and conform in outward behavior even as they are troubled within; to each, it looks like he or she is the only one who disagrees. Writ large to the totalitarian state, the support of a majority of the population is unnecessary. The appearance of support will suffice.

The mechanisms that generate the illusion of unanimity operate within science, medicine, and journalism as well as among the general public. Some conform enthusiastically to the orthodoxy; others complain in whispers to sympathetic colleagues. Those who voice dissent publicly become radioactive. The consequences of their apostasy (excommunication from funding, ridicule in the media, shunning by colleagues who must "distance themselves," and so forth) serve to silence other potential dissidents, who prudently keep their views to themselves.

Notice that here I have not yet said what I personally think about vaccine safety, efficacy, or necessity (be patient); nonetheless, what I have said is enough for anyone to distance themselves from me to keep safe. If I'm not an anti-vaxxer myself, I certainly have their cooties.

Someone on an online forum that I cohost related an incident. His children had a playdate scheduled at their friend's house. A parent called him to ask if his family had been vaccinated. Politely, he said no, and his children were immediately disinvited.

While this parent doubtless believed he was being scientific in canceling the invitation, I doubt science was really the reason. Even the most Covid-orthodox person understands that the nonsymptomatic children of nonsymptomatic parents pose negligible risk of infection; furthermore, since vaccine believers presumably trust that the vaccine provides protection, rationally speaking they have little to fear from the unvaccinated. The risk is vanishingly small, but the moral indignation is huge.

Many if not most people get the vaccine in an altruistic civic spirit, not because they personally fear getting Covid, but because they believe they are contributing to herd immunity and protecting others. By extension, those who refuse the vaccine are shirking their civic duty; hence the epithets "filth" and "assholes." They become the identifiable representatives of social decay, ready for surgical removal from the body politic like cancer cells all conveniently located in the same tumor.

Social stability depends on people rewarding altruism and deterring antisocial behavior. These rewards and deterrents are encoded into morals and then into norms and taboos. Performing the rituals and avoiding the taboos of the tribe, and shaming and punishing those who do not, one rests serenely in the knowledge of being a good person. As an added benefit, one distinguishes oneself as part of the moral majority, a full member of society, and not part of the sacrificial minority. Our fear of nonconformity is born of ancient experience so deeply ingrained it has become an instinct. It is hard to distinguish it from morality.

The fear operating in the ostracism of the unvaxxed is mostly not fear of disease, though disease may be its proxy. The main fear, old as humanity, is of a social contagion. It is fear of association with the outcasts, coded as moral indignation.

In any society some people are especially zealous in enforcing group norms, values, rituals, and taboos. They may be controlling types, or they may simply care about the common good. They serve an important function when the norms and rituals are aligned with social and ecological health. But when corrupt forces hijack the norms through propaganda and the control of information, these good folks can become instruments of totalitarian control.

Those doing the scapegoating may honestly, even fervently, believe the narrative of "the unvaccinated endanger others." Again, while I find the evidence to the contrary persuasive, I won't try to build a case for it beyond the hints I've offered already. As the saying goes, you can't reason someone out of a position they didn't reason themselves into to begin with. Furthermore, most of the citations I would use would come from blacklisted sources, which, owing to their heresy, are unacceptable to those who trust official sources of information. If you trust the official sources, why then, you trust their exclusion of the heretical information. When official sources exclude all dissent, then all dissent becomes a priori invalid to those who trust them.

Consequently, much of the dissent migrates to dodgy right-wing websites without the resources to check facts and scrutinize sources. One would think, for example, that a highly credentialed scientist like Dr. Peter McCullough, a professor of medicine, author of hundreds of peer-reviewed articles, and president of the now-disbanded Cardio Renal Society of America, would be able to find a hearing outside the right-wing media ecosystem. But no. He's been sidelined to places like the right-wing Catholic *John-Henry Westen Show*.[7] I wish I could find a link to this persuasive interview somewhere else, especially because there is actually nothing right wing about McCullough's views.

Tragically, the sites that host people like McCullough are quite often home to anti-immigrant and anti-LGBTQ articles that use the same tactics leveled at anti-vaxxers, tap into the same template of dehumanization and scapegoating, and lend themselves to the same fascistic ends.

Moving the Masses

For these reasons, I won't try too hard to substantiate my belief that—and I may as well say it explicitly as a gesture of goodwill to the censors, who will thus have an easier time deciding what to do with this article—the Covid vaccines are much more dangerous, less effective, and less necessary than we are told. They also seem not as dangerous, at least in the short term, as some fear. People are not dropping dead in the streets or turning into zombies; most of my vaccinated friends seem to be just fine. So it is hard to know. The science on the issue is so clouded by financial incentives and systemic bias that it is impossible to rely on it to light a way through the murk. The system of research and public health suppresses generic medicines and nutritional therapies that have been demonstrated to greatly reduce Covid symptoms and mortality, leaving vaccines as the only choice. It also fails to adequately investigate numerous plausible mechanisms for serious long-term harm. Of course, plausible does not mean certain: At this point no one knows, or indeed can know, what the long-term effects will be. My point, however, is not that the anti-vaxxers are right and being unjustly persecuted. It is that their persecution enacts a pattern that has little to do with whether they are right or wrong, innocent or guilty. The unreliability of the science underscores that point, and suggests that we take a hard look at the deadly social impulses that the science cloaks.

To say that official sources exclude *all* dissent overstates the case. In fact, peer-reviewed publications and highly credentialed medical doctors and scientists concur with much of what I've said. Admittedly, they are in the minority. But if they were right, we would not easily know it. The mechanisms for controlling *mis*information work equally well to control *true* information that contradicts official sources.

The foregoing analysis is not meant to invalidate other explanations for Covid conformity: the influence of Big Pharma on research, the media, and government; reigning medical paradigms that see health as a matter of winning a war on germs; a general social climate of fear, obsession with safety, the phobia and denial of death; and, perhaps most importantly, the long disempowerment of individuals to manage their own health.

Nor is the foregoing analysis incompatible with the theory that Covid and the vaccination agenda is a totalitarian conspiracy to surveil, track, inject, and control every human being on Earth. There can be little doubt that some kind of totalitarian program is well underway, but I have long believed it an emergent phenomenon agglomerating synchronicities to fulfill the hidden myth and ideology of Separation, and not a premeditated plot among human conspirators. Now I believe both are true; the latter subsidiary to the former, its avatar, its symptom, its expression. While not the deepest explanation for humanity's current travail, conspiracies and the secret machinations of power do operate, and I've come to accept that some things about our current historical moment are best explained in those terms.

Whether the totalitarian program is premeditated or opportunistic, deliberate or emergent, the question remains: How does a small elite move the great mass of humanity? They do it by aggravating and exploiting deep psycho-social patterns such as Girardian sacrificial violence. Fascists have always done that. We normally attribute pogroms and genocide to racist ideology, the classic example being anti-Semitic fascism. From the Girardian perspective it is more the other way around. The ideology is secondary: it is a creation and a tool of impending violent unanimity. Sacrificial violence creates its necessary ideological conditions. The same might be said of slavery. It was not that Europeans thought Africans were inferior and so thus enslaved them. It was that thinking them inferior was required *in order* to enslave them.

On an individual level, too, who among us has not operated from unconscious shadow motivations, creating elaborate enabling justifications and ex post facto rationalizations of actions that harm others?

Why is fascism so commonly associated with genocide, when as a political philosophy fascism is about unity, nationalism, and the merger of corporate and state power? It is because fascism needs a unifying force powerful enough to sweep aside all resistance. The *us* of fascism requires a *them*. The civic-minded moral majority participates willingly, assured that fascist policies are for the greater good. Something must be done. The doubters go along too, for their own safety. No wonder today's authoritarian institutions know, as if instinctively, to whip up hysteria toward the newly minted class of deplorables, the anti-vaxxers and unvaccinated.

Fascism taps into, exploits, and institutionalizes a deeper instinct. The practice of creating dehumanized classes of people and then murdering them is older than history. It emerges again and again under all political systems. Our own is not exempt. The campaign against the unvaccinated, garbed in the white lab coat of Science, munitioned with biased data, and waving the pennant of altruism, channels a brutal, ancient impulse.

Does that mean that the unvaccinated will be rounded up in concentration camps and their leaders ritually murdered? No, they will be segregated from society in other ways. More importantly, the energies invoked by the scapegoating, dehumanizing, pollution-associating campaign can be applied to gain public acceptance of coercive policies, particularly policies that fit the narrative of removing pollution. Currently, a vaccine passport is required to visit certain countries. Imagine needing one to go shopping, drive a car, or exit your home. It would be easily enforceable anywhere that has implemented the "internet of things," in which everything from automobiles to door locks is under central control. The flimsiest pretext will suffice once the ancient template of sacrificial victim, the repository of pollution, has been established.

René Girard was, from what I've read of his work, something of a fundamentalist. I do not agree with him that *all* desire beyond mere appetite is mimetic or that *all* ritual originates in sacrificial violence, powerful though these lenses are. By the same token, I don't want to reduce our current acceleration toward techno-totalitarianism and a biosecurity state to just one psycho-social explanation, however deep. Yet it is important to recognize the Girardian pattern, so we know what we are dealing with, so that we can creatively expand our resistance beyond futile debate over the issues—and most importantly, so we can identify its operation within ourselves. Any movement that leverages contempt in its rhetoric fits the Girardian impulse. Elements of scapegoating such as dehumanization, rumor-mongering, stereotyping, punishment-as-justice, and mob mentality are alive within dissident communities as they are in the mainstream. Any who ride those powers to victory will create a new tyranny no better than the previous.

There is another way and a better future. I will describe it in the final essay of the Girard series, although the reader already knows what it is, by feel if not in words. This future reaches into the present and the past to show itself anytime that vengeance gives way to forgiveness, enmity to reconciliation, blame to compassion, judgment to understanding, punishment to justice, rivalry to synergy, and suspicion to laughter. Transcendence is in the human being.

The Sacrificial King

SEPTEMBER 2021

While this essay is not essential to the thesis of the Girard series, it adds more flavor to the pot. I didn't know where else in the series to put the material around ritual regicide, but it was too fun to leave out. So I made it into a short, stand-alone essay.

It is not wholly irrelevant, of course. Lately I have vacillated between two states. Sometimes I feel sure that resistance to the Covid regime is going to win, has already won. Other times I abide in the crushing feeling of accelerating doom, when it seems that the propaganda machine is unstoppable. When I am in the former state, which is the dominant one, I know that since we have already won, the important issue will be the manner of our victory. Will it fall into the same pattern of ritually sacrificing the elites who we blame for the problem? Will we reenact the usual pattern of retributive justice—which expresses the same destroy-the-enemy mentality as germ-based medical thinking? In addition to being entertaining, this essay means to forestall that scenario.

Sacrificial victims are proxies for disorder, pollution, and evil. In normal times they come from various marginal and powerless minorities. In revolutionary times, the class of sacrificial subjects flips to those who stand apart by standing above. The bloodshed of revolutionary France, Russia, China, Cambodia, and others, where the liquidation of the old elites surpassed any practical need of power, echoed ancient precedent and could well be repeated if we remain blind to its ritual motivation.

Evidence from literature and anthropology suggests that in many societies, the original sacrificial victim was the king. As the one responsible for the well-being of the nation, if ever calamity befell it, the king would be the natural choice to represent order-turned-to-chaos. In some places, he would be required to commit all manner of forbidden acts so as to concentrate poison within himself. If misfortune befell the realm, his sacrifice would remove the poison, appease the gods, and restore harmony to the realm. Or his timely sacrifice could forestall calamities like floods, famines, or plagues from happening.

One might imagine that the king was not always enthusiastic about ritual regicide. He might have suggested, "Don't sacrifice me, let's sacrifice this criminal over here." Eventually substitutes were found, such as prisoners or children, or animals (a literal scapegoat, for instance), or various kinds of effigies. Or a special temporary king would reign in unrestrained debauchery for the duration of a festival, which concluded with his sacrifice (and therefore the symbolic removal of his sins from society). The carnival king often took the form of a fool or a buffoon, someone to display human faults, foibles, and failings in exaggerated form. One cannot help but wonder at the latent psycho-social forces that propelled Donald Trump to power and then tore him down again. His personality suited him perfectly to the role, foreshadowed by his pro wrestling persona, of carnival king. Ostentatious excess is part of the job description.

The perennial impulse of ritual regicide has also surfaced in recent times at Burning Man, whose king—an effigy of sorts— perishes by immolation at the festival's conclusion. Another faint vestige of this practice is the homecoming king and queen and the prom king and queen, though they are not, in contemporary American culture, ritually murdered. Or are they? They are in fact favorite targets of gossip. A primal impulse lurks in the human psyche to tear down our rulers; hence our fascination with celebrity scandals. Something is at work here deeper than displaced proletarian anger or the revolutionary instinct of the oppressed. It is a rebellion against order itself, and a hunger for the renewal that follows the descent into chaos.

This does not bode well for today's elites. Whatever their faults, the technocracy, billionaires, and political leadership are creations of a system more than they are its architects. They play the roles our reigning systems and paradigms cast for them. They are today also conforming to the requirements of another, more ancient role: that of the evil king, fit for sacrifice. To requote S. Mark Heim: "They are accused of the worst crimes the group can imagine, crimes that by their very enormity might have caused the terrible plight the community now experiences."[1] Not only do the people naturally impute such crimes to their elites, but the elites seem inexorably drawn to depravity. Power and depravity seem to go hand in hand; when scandal erupts, we are rarely surprised. A modern rendition of the evil king archetype is found in the theory that a satanic cult pervades the power elite, who commit unspeakable acts in private as they plot to further enslave the world. Whatever the objective truth behind this mythologizing, our leaders are, at least in perception, starting to take on the necessary attributes of the anti-king, to serve as symbols of concentrated pollution which can be excised from the body politic.

"Others loudly proclaimed that the evil spirit had been loosed upon the populace by the priests themselves." At the present writing the wall of denial is crumbling around what has seemed likely to many observers from the start: that SARS-CoV-2 is a genetically engineered virus. For the past year we have been assured that that was a "debunked conspiracy theory," a "pants-on-fire lie," and endured censorship for broaching the idea on social media. We saw renegade scientists like Judy Mikovits ridiculed for claims about gain-of-function research—claims that mainstream media is finally entertaining. Now we see stirrings of the rage that betrayal spawns, and imputations of "the worst crimes the group can imagine." A quarter of the public believes the virus was *deliberately* released.[2] Millions also think vaccines are a stealth eugenics technology and believe the above-mentioned theory that a satanic human-trafficking cult controls the world. These myths are difficult to prove or to falsify. From the Girardian perspective their objective factuality doesn't matter, just as it doesn't matter whether, as in some societies, the sacrificial king carried out the taboo deeds he was required to perform, or, as in other societies, he performed symbolic substitutes for those deeds. What was important was that he occupied the mythic role.

Whether they are guilty of some, all, or none of the heinous acts attributed to them, when we topple our elites in the name of justice, let us be aware that something wilder and more primal than justice is being served. A few sacrificial victims may slake the mob's thirst, but that won't bring about systemic change. Indeed, the rite of sacrifice is what keeps systems in place.

Let us remember that in coming times. The toppling of statues by protesters may well prefigure the real thing, a paroxysm of popular violence against the elites who seem to have betrayed us. Especially in the United States, our governing institutions float atop a seething lava pit of resentment that requires only a triggering incident to erupt. For decades now it has been directed mostly inward and at each other, as rising levels of depression, chronic disease, addiction, divorce, suicide, and civil strife demonstrate. The institutions' control of information keeps a lid on this volcanic rage for the time being, but the social order is precarious. Any number of disasters or revelations could breach the container of information control. But if all that happens is to take vengeance on the elites, little will change.

The autocracy of prerevolutionary France was followed by the autocracy of Napoleon. The autocracy of czarist Russia was followed by that of Stalin. The liquidations of the elites cleared the way for new actors to occupy the same roles. We can do better than that. The time has come for a different kind of revolution.

To those who equate "something must be done" to violence, not taking vengeance seems like inaction. Certainly, those who falsified data, censored dissent, suppressed inexpensive treatments, and manipulated the public should be removed from positions of trust, but must we replicate the age-old pattern of sacrificial violence, which never looks at the context of those deeds but rather symbolically transfers the poison from the system to its functionaries?

We need not. We can transcend the "deeper instinct" that turns human beings toward vengeance, punishment, and violence. Is that really an instinct after all? Could we build society around other instincts: the instinct for compassion, forgiveness, and reconciliation?

A Temple of This Earth

SEPTEMBER 2021

Many of the people who were heartened by "Mob Morality and the Unvaxxed" were a little disappointed by this essay. Superficially, especially those with a militant position against vaccines, it seems to strike a conciliatory tone. Read it closely—it does not equivocate about the mob phenomenon unfolding today. What it does, which many find disturbing, is to turn that lens back on the health freedom movement and ask, "In what ways are we too deploying the very tools of oppression wielded against ourselves?"

I believe the forces of health freedom are going to win the present conflict. What concerns me is the manner of the victory. Will it be merely a turning of the tables, in which the punishing of the former oppressor sets in motion the same patterns of domination from which we are trying to free ourselves? Isn't that a higher-level example of the Girardian pattern—rivalry between factions, reciprocal violence, and vengeance?

The real revolution is to transcend that pattern altogether. That transcendence has been a major theme of my work starting with my book The More Beautiful World Our Hearts Know Is Possible, *or even before. That is where this essay lands, drawing on Christian and Buddhist theology to move beyond what theologian Walter Wink called "redemptive violence." It is a message profoundly disturbing to militant partisans for whom the goal of glorying over the demise of a humiliated enemy has stealthily usurped the original goal of their movement.*

Before they send their opponents off to the guillotine, they should remember that the defeated elites are never its final victims. Always, eventually, its insatiable thirst claims the revolutionaries themselves.

The purpose of this Girard essay series is to illuminate a path toward the transcendence of the ancient pattern that René Girard called sacrificial violence, in which society discharges its rage, its anxiety, and its rivalries upon a dehumanized victim class. This latent force swells in times of social stress as in an economic crisis, famine, plague, or political upheaval. Then elite powers can hijack it toward fascistic ends.

In part 3 of this series, "Mob Morality and the Unvaxxed," I looked at the stigmatization and ostracism of the unvaccinated as a conspicuous current example of mob dynamics in action. Yet mob dynamics far transcend the vaccine issue, and in fact operate among vaccine dissidents as well, whose thought patterns sometimes mirror those of the orthodoxy: We are the good guys, they are the bad guys. We are rational, they are irrational. We are conscious, they are asleep. We are ethical, they are corrupt. Neither this nor any dissident movement is exempt from the systemic poison of incivility that now pervades the body politic.

Self-righteousness, ridicule, name-calling, and contempt are necessary precedents to Girardian scapegoating. They are also powerful rhetorical and psychological tools to create solidarity among the troops. They imply: Deviate from our beliefs and we will ridicule you, too. Humans know as if instinctively the danger that follows ridicule and ritual humiliation by the group. It's an ancient pattern. First the crowd jeers and mocks the victim, then it smears her with shit. She is made contemptible, disgusting. Then the stones fly.

Such tactics might discipline the ranks and intimidate a portion of the fence-sitters into cooperation. I remember, before I became conscious of this tactic, feeling superior when I read something contemptuous of the wrong (that is, those the author disagreed with). Beneath the superiority were feelings of inclusion and safety. In fact I might even agree *in order* to feel superior, included, and safe. The tactic amounts to: "Do you want to be a good person and not contemptible? Then agree with me!"

The tactic is counterproductive when addressing those who hold firm opposing opinions. The contempt, rightly seen as an attack, drives them to circle the wagons and counterattack with the same weapon. Many of the undecided are repelled, too, as they see that something operating besides reason and a genuine desire to seek truth through dialog. It is a fight; more broadly, it is a war. In war both sides serve victory, not truth, however they may pretend otherwise.

A saying goes, "Truth is the first casualty of war." And the primal lie of war is the same as that of mob violence, the pogrom, and the witch hunt: that certain people are not fully human. As long as we perpetuate that lie, humanity will continue the tragic historical pattern. We will also remain befuddled in our personal and collective sensemaking.

This last point may not be obvious. So, at the risk of provoking the censor, I will use the vaccine controversy to illustrate how dehumanization blinds us to truth. On the vaccine skeptic side, the idea that virologists and other researchers are clueless, corrupt, delusional, or incompetent prevents skeptics from engaging the substance of mainstream scientific knowledge. They may credulously accept as fact speculative or easily debunked theories, failing to distinguish them from more robust claims. This sows confusion in the ranks.

Here is an example: the canard, common in some quarters of the vaccine skeptic community, that "No virus for Covid has been isolated and proven to exist according to Koch's postulates." While technically true, this represents an impossible demand. Koch's postulates were formulated for bacteria, which can (often) be grown on a nonliving medium and therefore "purified." Viruses can be grown only in living cells; therefore any sample with viral particles will also contain cell debris, including nonviral DNA and RNA. That is why combinatoric methods are used to establish the viral genome. To believe that hundreds of thousands of virologists have spent the last fifty years studying a hallucination, one must think they are corrupt fools unable to see the obvious. Viewing them that way prevents communication, learning, and a mutual quest for truth. It also draws attention away from more legitimate, more nuanced challenges to conventional paradigms of virology and vaccine science.* Orthodox scientists, fed up with ignorant challenges, harden their paradigms against more legitimate ones.

Tarring the whole skeptic movement with the wide brush proffered by its most unreasonable members, the pro-vaccine side often assumes the vaccine skeptics are a bunch of rabid zealots who care only about their own "freedom" at the expense of public health. How much attention will they give, then, to the whistle-blowers, dissenting scientists, and horrifying vaccine damage stories that may not make it onto official databases?

I saw graphic illustration of this deafness today as I perused some Instagram and TikTok channels by people who claim to be injured by vaccines. They report things like weeks of tremors that began shortly after vaccination, paralysis from the waist down, strokes, speech loss, and other debilitating misery. Often they report that their doctors say it is coincidence and has nothing to do with the vaccine. They seem sincere to me—but certainly

---

* In fact, in my view there are serious flaws in the standard paradigm of germ theory, which focuses on pathogens as the prime cause of infectious disease. While that lens offers insight, it leaves crucial issues in the shadows, such as coevolution between germ and host, symbiosis, beneficial gene transfer, and the benefits of immune challenge. Particularly neglected is terrain theory, which looks at the bodily conditions under which disease flourishes, and which standard thinking reduces to a simplistic matter of immunity and resistance.

not to many. The comment threads are profuse with hate. "Fake," "clown," and "liar" are some of the more mild comments. "Nut job." Threats to have Child Protective Services take their kids away. Misogynistic slurs (the majority of the posters are women). Yes, it is conceivable that these people are faking it, but how are the commentators so sure? How is Instagram so sure these posts are "harmful false information" when it takes them down? (Along with the comment threads, which contain similar stories of adverse events unacknowledged by doctors. Some Instagram channels, since removed, contained hundreds or thousands such stories.) Furthermore, since this suppression is institutionalized, how can we as a collective know if vaccine harm is indeed widespread? The failure of communication keeps us in the dark.

Censorship, disinformation, and propaganda have a crucial ally without which they would never be effective. The ally is mob psychology and the social habit of dehumanization. These tactics work only when we are ready to see others as the propaganda says we should, and don't try to find out for ourselves by actually listening to them.

The Enemy in Our Midst

It is unsurprising that the tendency to dehumanize others makes us vulnerable to propaganda. When we dehumanize, we are not in truth (since the truth is that each human being is a divine soul, is life itself, is a feeling, thinking subject with a unique experience of the world). When we are not in truth, we are vulnerable to lies.

We also become vulnerable to internal division and paranoia. Those attuned to villains and crooks everywhere are quick to see them in their own ranks. Then, all it takes to destroy a dissident movement is to start accusing certain members of being infiltrators, quislings, or "controlled opposition." These accusations exploit existing rivalries—"Aha! You disagree with me because you are a _____." Any movement that sees the world through a polarizing lens is prone to schisms itself.

None of this is to deny the existence of infiltrators and informants. The intelligence services have a long, documented history of infiltrating and attempting to destroy dissident movements (such as the civil rights, environmental, and anti-globalization movements). Doubtless they are doing the same today with Covid policy dissenters. My message here is not to automatically trust everyone. Trust can come from a new foundation: I trust those who demonstrate a willingness to release their identity as good and right.

Let us also not deny that there is such a thing as corruption, as unconsciousness, ignorance, and irrationality. However, no human being can be reduced to any of those traits without obliterating their humanity and thus doing violence to the truth. Ultimately, violence to the truth leads to other forms of violence. To reduce someone to a degrading label short-circuits the question that is the sole deliverance of humanity at the present juncture: What is it like to be you?

The biggest crisis facing humanity today is not vaccines or their resistors; it is not infectious disease, chronic disease, overpopulation, or nuclear weapons. It is not even climate change. The biggest crisis today is a crisis of the word. It is a crisis of agreement. It is a Babelian crisis of communication. With coherency among us, no other problem would be hard to solve. As it stands, the prodigious powers of human creativity cancel each other out. The crystalline matrix of our co-creation has burst into shards. Why? It is not from lack of skill in communicating. It is from a habit of perception, a way of seeing each other that makes us less than what we are.

Before I proceed, let me make it clear that compassion does not equal capitulation. Communication does not equal compromise. Pacifism does not equal passivity. Seeing another person's divinity does not equal letting them have their way. Listening to other views does not equal keeping silent about one's own.

Contrary to what the partisan fears, humanizing the opponent makes us more effective, not less, in serving goals that must ultimately unite us all: healing, justice, and peace. Even if it comes to a fight, one will fight better free of delusions about the enemy.

To take a totally random example, ahem, let's say I want to stop the technocratic plan, spearheaded by Bill Gates, to monitor, inject, track, and control every human on Earth and feed their biometric data, movement data, and real-time physiological data into a centralized database that can then issue privileges and restrictions that keep everyone safe. To stop this from happening, I'd better understand *why* it is happening. If I tell myself it is because Bill Gates & Co. are gibbering fiends bent on making others suffer, there is a lot I will not see. I will be blind to the reasons why such people are so enamored of technology to begin with. I won't look at the implicit mythology that equates progress with control. I won't look at cultural patterns of domination. All the while, I will be fighting a caricature and not the enemy himself.

For all I know, Bill Gates fervently believes he is working for the good of humanity. He is convinced of his public identity as a philanthropist—a lover of humanity. His heart swells with righteous certitude. He has ready justifications for certain things he's done that even he knows were wrong. Some things, maybe, he just prefers not to think about. In short, maybe he isn't that different from you or me. I can and do reject utterly his vision of the future; therefore I think he is a dangerous individual. But an evil one? I cannot know that. Why would I be so sure? Conditioned by the Hollywood myth of the Villain, I might be tempted to see him that way. But won't I oppose him more effectively if I am aware of his real psychology, or at least willing to look for it? To do that, though, I have to be willing to see him as fully human. This does not mean to be soft and let him have his way. Quite the opposite. We will be more effective, not less, in standing up to oppression of any kind when we understand the nature of our oppressors and stop misattributing their actions to "evil." In so doing, we open the possibility that they will rehumanize us as well, and that something other than the victory of one group over another will determine the future.

This still applies even if some people *are* evil. Surely there are some truly psychopathic individuals among the elites, but even normal people, under the intoxication of ideology and power, can carry out heinous policies. Conversely, one cannot assume that just because most scientists and policymakers are decent people that they are immune to the contagion of mob psychology. Mob psychology organizes beliefs and actions around its dictates, generating endless rationalizations, justifications, and pretexts. Good people can do evil things, all the while firmly convinced of their righteousness. In order to speak to such people, we have to learn to question the subject of their righteousness without denying their decency.

Now is not the time to demur and keep our heads down. It is time to stand up and speak out, and our words will be more powerful if we speak to the real human beings underneath our assumptions about them.

Transcendence from the West

The late philosopher René Girard argued that the arc of reciprocal violence relieved by violent unanimity spawned human ritual, culture, and religion. Yet, it is in religion that we may find our deliverance from the pattern, from the diversion of revolutionary energy into round after round of scapegoating.

I'll offer an example from East and West. First, West. The Christ story at first glance seems to fit the mold of the sacrificial victim, but in fact it breaks it. Scapegoating depends on associating the victim with pollution of some kind, so that the pollution can then be removed. Christian teaching insists on the sinlessness of Jesus, his purity and divinity. Faced with an unruly crowd and ruling a land riven by social tensions, Pontius Pilate knew what to do: offer a victim to the mob. Typically, the peace that would follow would prove the righteousness of the slaughter. But the Jesus story doesn't play out as usual. Unlike in most myths (Batman subdues Joker and saves Gotham; Superman kills Lex Luthor and saves the world; the Avengers kill Thanos and save the universe; politicians save us from terrorists and the uneducated), in this story, the victim is the epitome of innocence. His innocence proclaims guilt to be irrelevant to the appetites of the mob. Therefore, Jesus's innocence bespeaks the innocence of everyone, even the guilty, who has ever been the mob's victim. For as S. Mark Heim puts it, "Any human being can be plausibly scapegoated and no human can prevail when the collective community turns against her."[1]

Forgiveness is the defining teaching of Christianity. Properly understood, forgiveness is not a kind of indulgence—you are bad but I forgive you anyway. Forgiveness comes from the flash of understanding: "If I were in the totality of your situation, I may well have done what you did." In other words, it comes from a felt recognition of our common humanity. This same understanding is what obviates judgment. Some of the most potent images in the Gospels are about forgiveness and judgment. Jesus on the cross says of his tormenters, "Forgive them Father, for they know not what they do." It isn't "Forgive them Father because you're a nice God and believe in second chances, so please go easy on them."

The horrors of the human condition cannot be blamed on a scattering of psychopaths. The sum total of millions of perfectly good intentions also ends in tragedy. Why? Because they know not what they do. In the crucifixion scene, what they do not know is that they are crucifying an innocent man. So it is always, when we victimize someone. Even if they are guilty of a crime, usually they are not guilty of all the dehumanized attributes affixed to them in the sacrificial process.

It is in the nature of organized religion that its institutions tend to enact the very opposite of its core esoteric principles. The core principle of the religion of science is humility; its institutional expression is arrogance. Likewise, Christianity has no rival in judging, condemning, dehumanizing, and scapegoating. That history is plain to see: the Inquisition, the witch hunts, the enslavement of Africans, the genocide of indigenous people, and the subjugation of women all happened under official church sanction. Nonetheless, the church's original teachings still call us toward the transcendence of such things. S. Mark Heim says:

133

Redemptive violence—the sort of violence that claims to be for the good of many, to be sacred, to be the mysterious ground of human life itself— always purports to be the means of overcoming sin (removing pollution, punishing the transgressor who has brought disaster on the community). The sin it characteristically claims to overcome is the offense of the scapegoat, the crime the victim has committed. But in the passion accounts the sin in view is that of the persecutors. It is not the sin of the one which jeopardizes the many, but the sin of the many against the one. In the passion narratives, redemptive violence stands forth plainly and unequivocally as itself the sin that needs to be overcome.[2]

Once the buildup to redemptive violence is complete, mere restraint is unlikely to stop it. We must start earlier and undo its underpinnings. We must interrupt habits of contempt, poisonous gossip, condemnation, psychological pathologizing, name-calling, and other forms of dehumanization. And we must stop seeing the world in terms of a fight. The fight, the war, is a lens that reveals little and obscures much. It casts reality into familiar tones—the tones of black and white, us and them, good and evil. That picture is familiar, addictive even. But for many of us it is no longer comfortable and feels no longer true. Partly it is futility, partly it is exhaustion that moves us to disengage from the debate, the campaign, the crusade. From that exhaustion and burnout and surrender, new possibilities are born.

Surrender does not mean capitulation to the other side. It is to stop seeing in terms of sides and framing issues in terms of who wins. It is to serve truth rather than victory. The lie behind judgment is "If I were you in the totality of your situation, I would have done differently." Do you ever really know that though? Or is that judgment based on a lie to yourself about what you think you know?

Transcendence from the East

The religious traditions of the East bear similar fruit from a different tree. The tree is the dissolving of rigid binary distinctions, especially that between self and other. The *Dao De Jing* (*Tao Te Ching*), for example, starts with a statement on the inexpressibility of absolute truth and, in its second verse, describes the mutual dependency and co-arising of opposites. But here I will invoke the Buddhist principle of interbeing.

Interbeing says that existence is relationship. It isn't just that we depend on each other, on the rainforests, on the sun, water, and soil to survive. It is that they are part of our very being. Accordingly, if a rainforest is cut down, or the small copse of trees near your home is removed, something of you dies as well. That is why the events happening on Earth today hurt so much. They are happening to each of us.

Interbeing says that outside and inside reflect and contain each other. A country that visits violence on the world will suffer domestic violence. A nation that locks up millions of its citizens cannot be free. No person can be fully healthy in a sick world. And the things we condemn the most in others live in some form within ourselves. The revered teacher Thich Nhat Hanh conveys this principle eloquently in his poem, "Please Call Me by My True Names." Here are a few stanzas:

> I am the child in Uganda, all skin and bones,
> my legs as thin as bamboo sticks,
> and I am the arms merchant,
> selling deadly weapons to Uganda.
>
> I am the twelve-year-old girl,
> refugee on a small boat,
> who throws herself into the ocean
> after being raped by a sea pirate,
> and I am the pirate,

my heart not yet capable
of seeing and loving.

I am a member of the politburo,
with plenty of power in my hands,
and I am the man who has to pay
his "debt of blood" to my people,
dying slowly in a forced labor camp.

My joy is like spring, so warm
it makes flowers bloom all over the earth.
My pain is like a river of tears,
so vast it fills the four oceans.

Please call me by my true names,
so I can hear all my cries and laughter at once,
so I can see that my joy and pain are one.

Please call me by my true names,
so I can wake up,
and the door of my heart
could be left open,
the door of compassion.[3]

If we are ever to transcend the human condition as we've known it, we have to start actually following the pleas of great teachers like Thich Nhat Hanh. The "true names" by which he wants to be called include my name and your name. Locating evil in others, then destroying them in hopes of destroying evil, we banish to the unconscious the parts of ourselves projected onto our enemies. There these shadows multiply, infiltrating life from within until the day when they seize command in a fit of violence.

The "door of compassion" is the dissolving of the barriers that separate. There is truth in "I am the girl. I am the pirate. I am the arms merchant." There is truth also in "I am not any of them," but while the latter truth is continually reinforced by modern ideology, systems, and economy, the truth of nonseparation gets lost. It is time to reclaim it. Does that mean we let pirates and arms merchants continue to ply their trade? Of course not. But we do not load onto them all the various evils we can imagine and hope to cleanse the world of evil by cleansing the world of pirates.

I would like to ask the partisans on all sides of the issues of our time to switch their allegiance. Not to the other side, but from victory to love. You may believe that your cause, for example the pro-vaccine cause or the anti-vaccine cause, is precisely love in action. And maybe it is. However, if ever you notice your side putting hate in service of the cause, you know that the primary allegiance is to winning.

One side may indeed win the battle by arousing disgust at the villains on the other side and casting them as demons, but they will have upped the level of disgust in the world, and society will be all the more vulnerable to manipulation and violence.

Do you hold healing above victory? Are you willing to accept a resolution in which society heals, but the evildoers are never punished and you are never vindicated? Where you never get the satisfaction of having been proved right all along? Where none of your opponents are ever sorry for what they did? Where you yourself might have to countenance your own error in something you held dear?

The Ring of Power

I was recently listening to a marvelous reading of J. R. R. Tolkien's *The Lord of the Rings* with my son Cary. In the book, Boromir suggests using the power of the One Ring against the dark lord Sauron. No, counsels Gandalf. If we do that and win, whoever wields the Ring becomes the new dark lord, because it is wholly evil. Someone then suggests hiding the ring, but Gandalf says no, it will be found again, and we are seeking victory over evil not just in our own age, but for the future, too.

Indulge me in this analogy. The One Ring is dehumanization. It is how dark powers rule this Earth: They induce us to dehumanize each other. It is indeed a mighty weapon, and we might indeed turn it against our rulers and overthrow them. But it isn't hard to imagine what the new rulers would be like, so sure they are in the right, so sure of the evil of those who oppose them, so practiced in the arts of ridicule and mockery, laughing at degrading caricatures of their opponents.

The wielder of the One Ring says, "Join me in the humiliation of the bad people." She invokes the power of the mob and unleashes it on her opponents. All for a good cause, the cause of freedom, the cause of justice, only to be used until good prevails at last. Unfortunately, she has fed the very monster she seeks to overthrow. She will always fear it. She will seek not to disband the mob but to direct it, lest she become its next sacrificial victim. The ring devours its wearer.

Let us instead cast the One Ring back into the fires whence it came. How? Through billions of everyday interactions, in private and public discourse. There is another instrument we can wield that is greater than dehumanization. We might call it love. Taking many forms, it draws on the truth of each other's divine humanness (the Christ) and our fundamental inseparability (interbeing). It can take the form of courtesy, of humor, or of reason. It can express anger without hate, responsibility without blame, and truth without self-righteousness. It opens others up to listen: Sensing they are not under attack, they feel less need to defend. By putting connecting ahead of convincing, love has the uncanny power to change minds far more effectively than any frontal assault of evidence and logic. To wield this instrument, we must be willing to be changed ourselves—that willingness is itself a powerful invitation. Without it, what reason have you to expect that anyone's mind will change? This is the kind of humility that results from seeing others in their full humanity. Through it we can reclaim the power of the word, the power of agreement, the power of coherency. Holding each other sacred, we will make a temple of this Earth.

Beyond Industrial Medicine

SEPTEMBER 2021

Like much of my writing during the Covid era, I wrote this essay in a burst of impatience. I was fed up—fed up with the narrowness of the debate around Covid, which through its tacit agreements about what to talk about and not talk about cements key assumptions into place. These assumptions need to be questioned.

I will confess to an ulterior motive in raising the example of glyphosate: I wanted to reestablish the connection between environmentalism and natural health. We will never extricate health from environment; fundamentally, what we do to the Earth, we do to ourselves. When industrial practices and mindsets damage the ecosystem, that damage unavoidably redounds to human health. And vice versa—for example, the poisoning of our bodies with antibiotics, birth control hormones, and so forth ends up poisoning soil and water, too.

One of the most distressing aspects of the Covid era has been the splitting apart of the Left, which originally included strong critiques both of industrial polluters and Big Pharma profiteers. The spectacle of ostensibly anti-authoritarian, anti-fascist leftists parading in support of the most entrenched corporate interests on the planet has dismayed a lot of old-time leftist radicals. In this and other essays, I hoped to recall environmentalists to their deeper principles, which will necessarily bring them to question medical totalitarianism, too.

L et's say I'm addicted to prescription painkillers. You are my concerned friend. "Charles," you say, "you've really got to get off this medication. It's ruining your health, and someday you're likely to OD."

"But I can't stop taking it. I'm in pain all the time. If I don't take it I can't function at all. I have terrible back pain, and my doctor says there is nothing I can do about it."

If you accept the premises of my response, you'll have little more to say. If we both accept that there is no other way to reduce the pain, and that the cause of the pain is incurable, then I'm right, I have to keep taking the painkiller.

Now let's talk about glyphosate, the much-maligned herbicide that Monsanto markets as Roundup. Critics make compelling points about its effects on human and ecological health. Defenders rebut those points, at least to the satisfaction of regulators. The debate has raged now for decades. One point that Roundup's defenders make is this: "Look, Roundup is the most effective broad-spectrum herbicide we have. If we stop using it, crop yields would fall. We would have to use other, less effective herbicides that might be even more toxic to human beings and the environment. Roundup is the safest, most economical option available."

Here again, if we accept these premises, we are nine-tenths of the way to conceding the argument. By limiting the debate to Roundup itself, its relative harms and benefits, we implicitly accept as a given the entire system of agriculture of which Roundup is a part. If we take for granted an industrial system of monocrop agriculture, then Roundup's defenders may be correct. We need Roundup, or something like it, to run the current system. If we don't change it, then banning Roundup will just result in a switch to other herbicides: new chemicals or genetic technologies that will have their own dangerous side effects.

Most critics of glyphosate are not motivated by the desire to replace it with another herbicide. Rather, glyphosate is a focal point for a critique of the entire system of industrial agriculture. If we had a system of small-scale, organic, regenerative, ecological, diversified, local agriculture, then glyphosate would not be much of an issue, because it would hardly be necessary. As I amply document in my book *Climate: A New Story*, this form of agriculture can outperform industrial agriculture in terms of yield per unit of land (although it requires more labor—more gardeners, more small farmers).

So do we need to keep glyphosate or not? If we take the current system of agriculture for granted, then maybe yes. But the conversation we need to be having is about the system itself. If we ignore that, then the glyphosate debate is a distraction. One might still oppose it on technical grounds, but the most powerful critique is not of the chemical itself, but of the system that requires it. The good folks at Monsanto probably take the system for granted, and cannot understand how their diligent efforts to make it work a little better are so misunderstood by environmentalists who cast them as villains.

The same pattern applies to what is called "mental health." Thirteen years ago I wrote an essay, "Mutiny of the Soul," which described mental conditions like depression and anxiety as forms of rebellion against an insane world. By calling those conditions illnesses and treating them with psychiatric medications, we suppress the rebellion and adjust the individual to fit society as it is.

If we accept society-as-it-is as right and good, then of course a maladjusted individual is a sick individual. If we also take as normal (or fail to see) conditions that make people unhappy, such as social isolation, unresolved trauma, the standard American diet, nature deficit, physical inactivity, or racial, economic, or other forms of oppression, then again we have little alternative but to adjust the individual. And if we exclude from consideration nonpharmacological forms of "adjustment," then we are left with drugs like SSRIs to alter brain chemistry.* Therefore, those who condemned "Mutiny of the Soul" and its sequel, "Mutiny of the Soul, Revisited," were perfectly correct within their frame of reference. They said things like "These drugs, while perhaps overused, are powerful and necessary interventions that have rescued many people from depression and allowed them to live normal lives." Leaving aside studies in which these drugs fail to outperform placebo, if we hold all other variables constant, one could reasonably argue that they are a beneficial technology, just as glyphosate is a beneficial technology in the context of industrial agriculture.†

In a similar vein, those who accept the basic goodness, rightness, or inalterability of the current system will see its critics as psychologically infirm. Quite a few people have, with the kindest of intentions and often quite gently, questioned me about whether my skepticism of vaccines and the mainstream medical system merely plays out unresolved childhood wounds around authority.

---

* Examples of nonpharmacological treatments for depression include psychedelic therapy, tai chi, Kundalini yoga, cold water immersion, red light therapy, pulsed electromagnetic field therapy, and many more. Wait, did I just give medical advice? Bad! I'm not suggesting any of these actually work. Nope. I'm just exercising my fingers. None of the above should be construed as medical advice. Please see your qualified medical practitioner before trying any of these. You are not qualified to do your own research. In fact, since life is increasingly medicalized, please don't do anything at all, even go outdoors, without permission of medical authority.

† To be clear, I think that even in the narrow terms of risks and benefits, both glyphosate and SSRIs are better left unused. That is due to their side effects, which the industry tends to cover up. In the case of SSRIs, these include all kinds of physical problems plus, quite possibly, murder and suicide. My point here is that there is an argument to be made for them that is at least worth having if we hold the system as unchangeable.

Am I rebelling against real injustice, or is medical authority a proxy for my father (who wouldn't let me stay up past my bedtime to watch *All in the Family*, the old tyrant). I might be suffering from oppositional defiant disorder (ODD). To those who accept medical authority as basically good and right, it seems reasonable that my suspicion of it must come from some kind of psychopathology.

The examples of glyphosate and SSRIs illustrate how perfectly decent people can participate in harm simply through their acceptance of the systems and realities that immerse them. Malice is a poor explanation. Certainly, ruthless, malicious, and psychopathic individuals are overrepresented among the global power elite. They thrive in our current system, rise to the top, and find ways to stay there. But their power depends on the deep stories I am describing here. They did not create those stories, but they feed them and feed off them.

This is one of the insights that launched my writing career. I spent fifteen years holding a single question in my mind: What is the origin of the wrongness? I found the aforementioned systems and realities to be products of ideologies so deeply woven into the fabric of civilization as to be nearly inseparable from it. Did some evil genius concoct the concept of the discrete, separate self marooned in an arbitrary universe of force, mass, atoms, and void? No, that mythology evolved organically, reaching its culmination in our time. It is in fact overripe, yet the fruit—the systems we inhabit and that inhabit us—has yet to fall from the tree. When it does it will split open and the seed of a new kind of civilization will grow.

Okay, Covid vaccines. We could argue about their relative harms and benefits, but again by thus narrowing the conversation we take for granted the system in which they naturally fit. Full disclosure: My personal opinion is that, even holding other variables constant, the risks and harms far outweigh the benefits. Last time I said that in an essay I got a lot of flak for not "documenting that claim," even though I said it was an opinion and not a claim. I'm not going to claim it now either, nor try to document it, (1) because many of the sources I would use are unacceptable to most of the people who disagree with me, and I would have to unfold a complex discussion of systemic bias in the information environment; (2) because my opinion draws heavily from practitioners in my circles who are seeing damage firsthand, and I can't cite them using publicly available documents; (3) most importantly, because right now I want to broaden the conversation to the system of industrial medicine, which bears close resemblance in many dimensions to the system of industrial agriculture. Also, since I'm not making false "claims," the scrupulously logical social media censors won't be able to unpublish this essay. Ha! Pwned!*

If we accept as a given the current state of public health along with reigning paradigms of modern medicine, then the case for vaccination is at least arguable, just as is the case for glyphosate in the context of industrial agriculture. (The case for *mandatory* vaccines is far weaker as the narrative of an "epidemic of the unvaccinated" crumbles and evidence mounts that the vaccines do not prevent infection or transmission but only lessen symptoms.) We could debate about relative harms, study designs, suppression of information by corporate interests, unlabeled ingredients, underreporting to the US government's Vaccine Adverse Event Reporting System (VAERS), and so on. But in engaging that particular debate, both sides implicitly agree *not* to talk about what lies outside its boundaries.

What lies outside the debate about vaccine safety? Effective natural and alternative treatments for Covid. Superiority of

---

* People keep telling me I made a typo here. "Pwned" is actually a term from video game culture, meaning to win a dominating victory over someone. I know that because I'm an avid gamer. Just kidding. I had and have teenage sons, which is why I'm so stylish and hip. That was a joke, too. Also, I was joking that my avoidance of making claims will balk the censors. Some people in the original comments section thought I was serious.

natural immunity to vaccine-induced immunity. The "terrain" of infection: Why some people experience serious illness and death, and others do not. The positive role viruses, even pathogenic ones, play in health and evolution. The decline of virulence over time. The sociological implications of handing body sovereignty over to government authorities.

Basically, vaccines are a way to keep society as we know it functioning as usual. The idea is, "Everybody get the jab and we can go back to normal." It is much like psychiatric medications. Taking for granted a society that makes vast numbers of people miserable, maybe we need those drugs to keep them happy, or at least functioning. They can get back to normal—the life defined by society's norms. Yet that life is what may have made them miserable to begin with. Similarly, what we have known as normal includes the conditions that result in needing (arguably, anyway) the jab in the first place.

Normal has been a society where autoimmunity, addiction, diabetes, obesity, and other chronic conditions are at epidemic levels.* This epidemic is actually quite new. In the 1950s, the prevalence of diabetes in the United States was a tenth what it is today. Obesity was a third. Autoimmune diseases were medical

---

* When I mention obesity I often get accused of "fat shaming." So let me say this: Obesity is not to be blamed on people's weak willpower or dumb choices. It is a function of childhood trauma, social programming, toxic environments, a social infrastructure in which physical activity is separated off into the category of "exercise," unmet needs that get displaced onto food, a food environment devoid of genuine nutrition, and many other factors. Sometimes overeating isn't involved. When it is, fat shaming is actually counterproductive as a way to get someone, especially oneself, to lose weight. That's because overeating (especially of sugar) can be a way to compensate for a lack of unconditional love and acceptance. It is when we love ourselves and each other exactly as we are, that that stage can be completed and change can happen. I made a small online course called Dietary Transformation to explore and practically integrate these and related ideas.

rarities. As most Covid deaths are in people with diabetes and other chronic conditions, the whole context of vaccine policy includes conditions that are historically aberrant.

Normal has been the disempowerment of people to maintain their own health themselves and in their community, making them dependent instead on experts to do things to them. The "patient" is passive, *patiently* enduring what the expert doctor does to her.

Normal has been a ubiquitous death phobia that worships at the altar of safety and would sacrifice anything for the promise of security, even at the cost of civil liberties, personal freedom, and community self-determination.

Normal has been the marginalization of holistic and natural healing modalities that offer effective treatments for Covid and most other conditions. Oops, that sentence will get this flagged as misinformation. Where's the data, Charles? Well that is part of the problem. Society has not devoted the vast resources into researching and developing herbal, nutritional, vibrational, and other unorthodox therapies that it has into pharmaceutical ones. They don't fit the funding system and they don't fit the paradigm. So evidence at the level of multiple large-scale double-blind placebo-controlled trials is scarce. Moreover, since many alternative therapies depend on unique relationships between therapist and patient, individualized treatments, or active work by the person being healed, they are inherently unsuitable for standardized trials. Standardized trials that produce the aforementioned "data" require the control of variables. They are part of what I've been calling industrial medicine—"industrial" is all about standardization, control, quantification, and scale.

That is not to say that alternative and holistic treatments for Covid or any other disease lack evidence. Far from it. But, to access their full power one must venture into realms beyond industrial paradigms and proofs.

I'd like to imagine, then, a different normal. It departs from industry's dream to remake the Earth, life, and the human being in its image. It is the normality of the age of ecology, the age of relationship, the age of community, the age of reunion.

In that future, it is normal to see health as a matter of good relationships within the body and outside it. Society redeploys the hundreds of billions it spends on sick care toward understanding and restoring these relationships. Every conceivable holistic, herbal, homeopathic, nutritional, energetic (and other) therapy is pursued, tried, tested, improved, and if effective, made available.

In that future, it also becomes normal to take responsibility for our own health and to receive support in doing that (because personal willpower is not enough, we are social beings and need support). The support is economic, legal, and infrastructural.

I asked my wife, Stella, an extremely effective healer, what she thinks health care could become. She said, "We recognize mind and body as a continuum. We don't see illness as a random misfortune. We know that resonant attention and the holding of space for emergent wholeness can heal, and that anyone can do this. We can return medicine to the people." I see Stella help people heal from real medical conditions nearly every day. Sometimes they are conditions doctors say are incurable. The power of these techniques (and so many others in the alternative world) is real, and they can be taught, and a new normal could be built on them.

Yes, we can return medicine to the people. The power to heal ourselves and each other has, like so much of modern life, been professionalized, turned into yet another set of goods and services. We can reclaim that power. The future of medicine is not high tech. Technology has its place (for example in emergency medicine), but it has usurped the place of other powers: the hand, the herb, the mind, the water, the soil, the sound, and the light. Can we imagine a health care system that fulfilled the promise of the medical alternatives that have touched millions of lives in the shadow of the conventional system? These alternatives should stop being alternative. Come on people, these actually work. They have gained momentum over the last half-century despite ridicule, marginalization, lack of funding, and persecution from mainstream institutions. They work. Let's take them seriously. We know how to be healthy. We remake society around that knowledge.

No authority during Covid has said, "People are sick, they need more time outdoors. People are sick, they need more touch. People are sick, they need healthy gut flora. People are sick, they need pure water. People are sick, they need less electromagnetic pollution. People are sick, they need less chemicals in food. People are sick, let's put diabetes warnings on soda pop. People are sick, let's encourage them to meditate and pray more. People are sick, let's get them in the garden. People are sick, let's make our cities walkable. People are sick, let's clean the air. People are sick, let's provide free mold remediation on all dwellings. People are sick, let's promote education about local herbs. People are sick, let's make the best supplements and practices of the biohackers and health gurus available to all. People are sick, let's heal our agricultural soils." None of these are as hard as keeping every human being six feet apart from every other. So let's do these things. Let's remake society in their image with as much zeal as we remade society in the year of Covid.

Am I saying not to talk about vaccines and focus only on the bigger picture? No. Vaccines, their dangers, their shortcomings, and the measures needed to coerce the unwilling are the visible tip of an iceberg, showing us starkly the system they represent. They are a window into a future of technological dependency where we put into our bodies whatever the authorities tell us to, and wonder why the promise of health, freedom, and a return to "normal" is always on the horizon but never here.

Another future beckons. It won't be handed to us by the same authorities and systems that rule today; we have to claim it. We claim it through the choices it offers. Which future does your next step lead toward? Toward more normalization of the world under control? Or toward the new normal I've described? The road has forked. It is time to choose.

The Rehearsal Is Over

OCTOBER 2021

For many years I have dimly foreseen the present convergence of crises: the unraveling, the civilizational initiation, the apocalyptic/ awakening. I have feared it and I have yearned for it. Now that it is here, two years in, still I can hardly believe it.

For much of 2020 I was in a state of semi-denial, alternating between vain, insincere hope that things would revert to normal, and despondent certainty that they would not and could not. From time to time, in the midst of this bipolar oscillation, came moments of clarity when I realized: This is the time we've been waiting for. I do not want the old normal to come back. Something new is possible. I've spoken of it for years—a more beautiful world—and it won't come by us sitting back and watching. It calls for our full participation. We've been preparing for this moment for a long time.

This essay along with another one not in this collection, "Time to Push," speaks from one of these moments of clarity. For most of my adult life, the breakdown in stories and systems was theoretical. Those of us who wrote about it helplessly joined the Debordian Spectacle—here were more things to stir the emotions as life went on as normal. Of course, the breakdown began long before 2020, and life for many was anything but normal, but for the majority everything still hung together. We were rehearsing in our minds for a play that we didn't fully expect to be performed. Now we are thrust onto the stage. The theoretical has become real. Life isn't going to return to normal, folks. A pretense of normal, maybe, will be offered you, but not one that you can stomach. Not one that leaves your soul intact. And that is good. Why else are we here, but to play the game of life for real?

A friend wrote me about her dilemma. She owns a company employing hundreds of people and is a staunch critic of that-which-shall-not-be-named. She said she has been trying to fly under the radar until sanity is restored, but with looming mandates for large employers, the radar will soon turn on her. What will she do?

I will share with you the inner monologue that her note provoked in me.

A return to sanity? Sanity will not be restored for us by others. We are the ones that must restore it. We cannot wait for others to be brave on our behalf. We are here in this initiatory moment to choose who we are. The choice of whether to capitulate or to act is a declaration: Who am I to be? What is the world to be? Am I serious enough about my vision for the world to risk my security for it? That is not a challenge meant to goad myself into action. It is simply true. Through my choice, I will know myself as I am. I will become as I choose. The rehearsal is over.

Many people trust the authorities and willingly comply with their rules. They face no dilemma, no initiatory moment, no self-defining world-creating choice point. Not yet.

But as the authorities' narratives devolve into absurdity and their rules devolve into oppression, more and more of us face this choice:

> To live your truth out loud, or
> To live by a lie, consoling yourself with secret protest.
> To do what you know is right, or
> To cave in to the pressure, consoling yourself with
> words you don't believe. "I had no choice."

Yes, for many of us it has come to such a choice. The rehearsal is over.

———

Maybe, I think, maybe now is not the time to be brave. Maybe now is not the time to speak out. I'll wait until it is a little safer.

But it will never be safe to be brave. Never.

If not now, when? If not I, who?

Shall I wait for others to do what I dare not do? We are ready. We've been preparing and being prepared for a long time. The rehearsal is over.

———

The message is not "Act now." Do not accept pressure, coercion, bribes or threats. Don't let me or anyone else tell you what to do or when to do it. We are fighting for the end of the time of dictating each other's choices, thinking I know better than you what *you* should be doing.

I trust you to know the right choice. Being trusted is an invitation to be trust*worthy*. Trusting you to be brave, you become brave, just as I become brave when people see me as brave. Bravery is not a personal achievement; it is a community function. It is a contagion. It is a mutual awakening.

Bravery means acting when you know it is time to act. It isn't the convenient time. It is simply the time. It is the moment of, "Enough!" It is the moment of, "It is time to do something about it." It is the moment of truth over consequences.

In that moment you act not because it is brave, but because it is necessary. You recognize that the moment has come. Why now? Because it is time. No other reason is needed.

Bravery means doing what is yours to do, when it is time to do it. Denying that knowing locks your heart in a box. Life becomes a chore. Despair descends like a fog, turning everything gray. Hope withers, leaving behind the dry empty husk called wishful thinking. And you face the dread of living the rest of life knowing, "I did not do what I was here to do, when the moment came and it counted."

The rehearsal is over.

———

If I am not brave, what reason have I to hope others will be? Courage and cowardice both are contagious. My choice establishes a principle of human nature. It declares not only who I am, but what a human being is and what the world shall be. Each choice is therefore a prayer. Our choices scaffold divine creation.

That is why synchronicity so often congeals around bravery. Synchronicity is the snapping of the laws of probability as reality shifts to align with brave choices.

Seeing that creative power, one knows the despair was based on false premises. The ego's cautious logic is reversed. The ego says, "Give me a guarantee that it will work and I'll be okay, then I'll do it." The ego says, "Promise me that other people will resist, and then I'll resist, too. Prove to me it won't be in vain. Guarantee that others will join in." God says, "Show me that you want a more beautiful world enough to actually risk something with no guarantee. Then you will see results beyond all reckoning."

Is your time for choosing here? You will recognize when it is. No one can escape that feeling of recognition when the moment comes. If you have read this far, that time is close. You know exactly what I'm talking about.

The rehearsal is over.

A Path Will Rise
to Meet Us

DECEMBER 2021

After all the many lenses through which I've viewed the goddess Covid, this one takes up the perspective of bullying and abuse. I explore how the bully or abuser can actually serve a developmental role for the victim, who must go through an inner transformation in order to exit the relationship. A curse becomes a blessing. A plague becomes a deliverance.

Might that also be true of the goddess Covid, which began as a literal plague? Will it provoke a positive transformation in human society? This final essay of this book leaves us where we began: at a crossroads. I cannot say what others will choose. Will we, collectively, repudiate the victim role we have occupied in relation to the world's ruling powers? Or perhaps it is better to ask: To what degree will we repudiate it?

As the pandemic narrative loses steam, that question will remain. Let us not be sanguine when the abuser apologizes and promises to do better next time. His nature is plain to see. Healing and redemption are possible only after victim and abuser abandon their roles. In my inner journey, this essay marked the moment where I was well and truly done with the false self-doubt that had muffled my voice. May it be so for all of us.

The first principle of non-violent action is that of non-cooperation with everything humiliating.
—MOHANDAS K. GANDHI

I once read an account of bullying in rural America in the early twentieth century. The narrator said, "If a victim did not stand up to them, there was no limit to how far the bullies would go." He described his schoolmates tying another child to the train tracks as a train approached (on the parallel track). There was no appeasing the bullies. Each capitulation only whetted their appetite for new and crueler humiliations.

The psychology of bullies is well understood: compensation for a loss of power, reenactment of trauma with roles reversed, and so forth. Beyond all that, though, the Bully archetype draws from another source. On some unconscious level, what the bully wants is for the victim to cease being a victim and to stand up to him. That is why submission does not appease a bully, but only invites further torment.

There is an initiatory possibility in the abuser-victim relationship. In that relationship and perhaps beyond it, the victim seeks to control the world through submissiveness. If I am submissive enough, pitiable enough, the abuser may finally relent. Other people might step in (the Rescuer archetype). There is nothing intrinsically wrong with submission or what improvisational theater pioneer Keith Johnstone called a low-status play. There are indeed some situations when doing that is necessary to survive. However, when the submissive posture becomes a habit and the victim loses touch with her capability and strength, the initiatory potential of the situation emerges. The bully or abuser intensifies the abuse until the victim reaches a point where the situation is so intolerable that she throws habit and caution to the wind. She discovers a capacity within her that she did not know she had. She becomes someone new and greater than she had been. That is a pretty good definition of an initiation.

When that happens, when the victim stands his ground and fights back, quite often the bully leaves him alone. On the soul level, his work is done. The initiation is complete. Of course, one might also say that the bully is a coward who wants only submissive victims. Or one might say that resistance spoils the sought-after psycho-drama of dominance and submission. There is no guarantee that the resistance will be successful, but even if it is not, the dynamics of the relationship change when the victim decides she is through being a victim. She may discover that a lot of the power the bully had was in her fear and not in the bully's actual physical control.

Until that shift happens, the situation is unlikely to change even if a rescuer intervenes. Either the intervention will fail, or the rescuer will become a new abuser. The world will ask again and again whether the victim is ready to take a stand.

Please do not interpret this as a cavalier suggestion to someone in an abusive relationship to simply "take a stand." That is easier said than done, and especially easy to say in ignorance of just what sort of courage would be required. In some situations, especially when children are involved, there is no way to resist without horrible risk to oneself or innocent others. Yet even in the most hopeless situations, the victim often learns a certain strength that she didn't know she had. Because submission often leads to further, intensifying violation, eventually she will reach her breaking point where courage is born. In that moment, freedom from the abuser is more important than life itself.

The relationship between our governing authorities and the public today bears many similarities to the abuser-victim dynamic. Facing a bully, it is futile to hope that the bully will relent if you don't resist. Acquiescence invites further humiliation. Similarly, it is wishful thinking to hope that the authorities will simply hand back the powers they have seized over the course of the pandemic. Indeed, if our rights and freedoms exist only by the whim of those authorities, conditional on their decision to grant them, then they are not rights and freedoms at all, but only privileges. By its nature, freedom is not something one can beg for; the posture of begging already grants the power relations of subjugation. The victim can beg the bully to relent, and maybe he will—temporarily—satisfied that the relation of dominance has been affirmed. The victim is still not free of the bully.

That is why I feel impatient when someone speaks of "When the pandemic is over" or "When we are able to travel again" or "When we are able to have festivals again." None of these things will happen by themselves. Compared to past pandemics, Covid is more a social-political phenomenon than it is an actual deadly disease. Yes, people are dying, but even assuming that everyone in the official numbers died "of" and not "with" Covid, casualties number one-third to one-ninth those of the 1918 flu; per capita it is one-twelfth to one-thirty-sixth.* As a sociopolitical phenomenon, there is no guaranteed end to it. Nature will not end it, at any rate; it will end only through the agreement of human beings that it has ended. This has become abundantly clear with the Omicron variant. Political leaders, public health officials, and the media are whipping up fear and reinstituting policies that would have been unthinkable a few years ago for

---

* Estimates of Spanish flu deaths range from ten million to fifty million. The global population was somewhat under two billion. In terms of life-years lost the contrast is even more stark. In the US in 1918–19, 99 percent of casualties were among people under sixty-five years of age, and half were among people age twenty to forty. The median age of death with Covid is around eighty.

a disease that, at the present writing, has reportedly killed one person globally. So we cannot speak of the pandemic ever being over unless we the people declare it to be over.

Of course, I could be wrong here. Perhaps Omicron is, as the World Medical Association chairman, Frank Ulrich Montgomery, has warned, as dangerous as Ebola.[1] Regardless, the question remains: Will we allow ourselves to be held forever hostage to the possibility of an epidemic disease? That possibility will never disappear.

Another thing I've been hearing a lot of recently is that "Covid tyranny is bound to end soon, because people just aren't going to stand for it much longer." It would be more accurate to say, "Covid tyranny will continue until people no longer stand for it." That brings up the question, "Am I standing for it?" Or am I waiting for other people to end it for me, so that I don't have to? In other words, am I waiting for the rescuer, so that I needn't take the risk of standing up to the bully?

If you do put up with it, waiting for others to resist instead, then you affirm a general principle of "waiting for others to do it." Having affirmed that principle, the forlorn hope that others will resist rings hollow. Why should I believe others will do what I'm unwilling to do? That is why pronouncements about the inevitability of a return to normalcy, though they seem hopeful, carry an aura of delusion and despair.

In fact, there is no obvious limit to what people will put up with, just as there is no limit to what an abusive power will do to them.

If the end of Covid bullying is not an inevitability, then what is it? It is a choice. It is precisely the initiatory moment in which the victim—that is, the public—discovers its power. At the very beginning of the pandemic I called it a coronation: an initiation into sovereignty. Covid has shown us a future toward which we have long been hurtling, a future of technologically mediated relationships, ubiquitous surveillance, big tech information control, obsession with safety, shrinking civil liberties, widening wealth inequality, and the medicalization of life. All these trends predate Covid. Now we see in sharp relief where we have been headed. Is this what we want? An automatic inertial trend has become conscious, available for choice. But to choose something else, we must wrest control away from the institutions administering the current system. That requires a restoration of real democracy; that is, popular sovereignty, in which we no longer passively accept as inevitable the agendas of established authority, and in which we no longer beg for privileges disguised as freedoms.

Despite appearances, Covid has not been the end of democracy. It has merely revealed that we were already not in a democracy. It showed where the power really is and how easily the facade of freedom could be stripped from us. It showed that we were "free" only at the pleasure of elite institutions. By our ready acquiescence, it showed us something about ourselves.

We were already unfree. We were already conditioned to submission.

In George Orwell's *1984*, Winston's interrogator O'Brien states: "The more the Party is powerful, the less it will be tolerant: the weaker the opposition, the tighter the despotism." The Covid era has seen endless indignities, humiliations, and abuse heaped upon the public, each more outrageous than the last. It is as if someone is performing a psychological experiment to see how much people are willing to take. Let's tell them that masks don't work, and then reverse it and require them to mask up. Let's tell them they can't shake hands. Let's tell them they can't go near each other. Let's shut down their churches, choirs, businesses, and festivals. Let's stop them from gathering for the holidays. Let's make them inject poison into their bodies. Let's make them do it again. Let's make them do it to their children. Let's censor their firsthand stories as "false information." Let's feed them obvious absurdities to see what they'll swallow. Let's make promises and break them. Let's make the same promises again and break them again. Let's require authorization for their every movement. Wow, they're still going along with it? Let's see how much more they will take.

I have written these lines as if the bullying powers were a bunch of cackling sadists who delight in the humiliation of their victims. That is not accurate. Most people staffing our governing institution are normal, decent human beings. While it is also true that these institutions are hospitable environments for martinets, control freaks, and sadists, more often they turn people *into* martinets, control freaks, and sadists. These individuals are more symptom than cause of the generalized abuse of the public today. They are functionaries, playing the roles that a systemically abusive drama requires. Causing suffering is not their root motivation, it is to establish control. The quest for power doubtless finds justification in the idea that it is all for the greater good. Yes, they think, it would be bad if evil people were in charge of the surveillance, censorship, and coercive apparatus, but fortunately it is we, the rational, intelligent, farseeing, science-based good guys who are at the helm.

Through the absolute conviction by those who hold power that they are the good guys, power transforms from a means to an end. As maybe it was to begin with—Orwell dispels the false justifications of power when he has O'Brien say:

> "The Party seeks power entirely for its own sake. We are not interested in the good of others; we are interested solely in power. Not wealth or luxury or long life or happiness: only power, pure power. What pure power means you will understand presently. We are different from all the oligarchies of the past, in that we know what we are doing. All the others, even those who resembled ourselves, were cowards and hypocrites. The German Nazis and the Russian Communists came very close to us in their methods, but they never had the courage to recognize their own motives. They

pretended, perhaps they even believed, that they had seized power unwillingly and for a limited time, and that just round the corner there lay a paradise where human beings would be free and equal. We are not like that. We know that no one ever seizes power with the intention of relinquishing it. Power is not a means, it is an end. One does not establish a dictatorship in order to safeguard a revolution; one makes the revolution in order to establish the dictatorship. The object of persecution is persecution. The object of torture is torture. The object of power is power. Now do you begin to understand me?"

The theme resumes on the next page:

He paused, and for a moment assumed again his air of a schoolmaster questioning a promising pupil: "How does one man assert his power over another, Winston?"

Winston thought. "By making him suffer," he said.

"Exactly. By making him suffer. Obedience is not enough. Unless he is suffering, how can you be sure that he is obeying your will and not his own? Power is in inflicting pain and humiliation. Power is in tearing human minds to pieces and putting them together again in new shapes of your own choosing. Do you begin to see, then, what kind of world we are creating?"

Thus it is that the privation, humiliation, and suffering of those they dominate is pleasing to the controllers. It isn't suffering *per se* that pleases them. They may even consider it a regrettable necessity. It pleases them as a hallmark of submission.

Covid-era policies cannot be understood merely through the lens of public health. In the Girard essays I explored Covid policies from the perspective of sacrificial violence, mob morality, dehumanization, and the exploitation of these by fascistic forces. Equally important is the perspective of power. Seeing Covid through the lens of rational public health, of course we should expect the "end of the pandemic" quite soon. Seeing through the lens of power, we cannot be so sanguine, any more than the bullied child can hope the bully will stop because, after all, "I've done everything he told me to."

The bully doesn't want the victim to do X, Y, and Z for their own sake. He wants to establish the principle that the victim will do X, Y, Z or A, B, or C on demand. That's why arbitrary, unreasonable, ever-shifting demands are characteristic of an abusive relationship. The more irrational the demand, the better. The controllers find it satisfying to see everyone dutifully wearing their masks. As with O'Brien, it is power, not actual public safety, that inspires them. That is why they roundly ignore science casting doubt on masks, lockdowns, and social distancing. Effectiveness was never the root motivation for those policies to begin with.

I learned about this, too, in school. In the senseless, degrading busywork and the arbitrary rules, I detected a hidden curriculum: a curriculum of submission.* The principal issued a series of trivial rules under the pretext of "maintaining a positive learning environment." Neither the students nor the administration actually believed that wearing hats or chewing gum impeded learning, but that didn't matter. Punishments were not actually for the infraction itself; the real infraction was disobedience. That is the chief crime in a dominance-submission relationship. Thus, when German police patrol the square with meter sticks to enforce social distancing, no one need believe that the enforcement will actually stop anyone from getting sick. The offense they

---

* The resemblance of school to lockdown society is uncanny. In school, one's movements are subject at all times to authorization. A hall pass is given for essential functions. And the top authority, superseding even the principal, is the doctor's note.

are patrolling against is disobedience. Disobedience is indeed offensive to the abusive party, and to anyone who fully accepts a submissive role in relation to it. When "Karens" report on their neighbors for having more than the permitted number of guests, is it a civic-minded desire to slow the spread that motivates them? Or are they offended that someone is breaking the rules?

It is uncomfortable for those who have knuckled under to a bully to see someone else stand up to him. It disrupts the idea of powerlessness and the role, which may have become perversely comfortable, of the victim. It invokes the initiatory moment by making an unconscious choice conscious: "I could do that, too." To resist the abuser asks others if they will resist, too. It is far from inevitable that they will accept the invitation, yet the example of courage is more powerful than any exhortation.

Today a wave of resistance to Covid policies is surging across the globe. You'll see little mention of it in mainstream media, but thousands and tens of thousands are protesting all across Europe, Thailand, Japan, Australia, North America . . . pretty much anywhere that lockdowns and vaccine mandates have been applied. People are risking arrest to defy lockdowns and curfews. They are walking out of jobs, losing licenses, enduring forced closures of their businesses, sometimes even losing custody of their children because they refuse to comply with vaccine mandates. They are getting kicked off social media for speaking out. They are sacrificing concerts, sports, skiing, travel, college, careers, and livelihoods. Under compulsory vaccination laws in Austria, they will soon risk prison.

Some people have much more to lose than others by speaking out, refusing vaccination, or engaging in civil disobedience. As someone who has relatively little to lose, it is not my job to demand other people be brave. It isn't anyone's job. We can, though, describe the reality of the situation. That fosters bravery, because it isn't only external fear, force, and threat that breeds submission. In an abusive relationship the victim often adopts some of the abuser's narrative: I am weak. I am contemptible. I am powerless. You are right. I am wrong. I need you. I deserve this. I am crazy. This is normal. This is okay.

When the victim internalizes the abuser, I say that the bandits have breached the castle walls. I know well what it is like to be a fugitive in my own castle, dodging the patrolling invaders to protect my secret sanity.

My understanding of the bullying victim comes from direct experience. I was among the youngest in my grade and reached puberty quite late. At age twelve I was a scrawny four-foot-ten-inch, ninety-pound weakling among the hulking adolescents of my former friend group. Their cruel jokes and torments were mostly not intended to cause physical pain, but rather to assert dominance and humiliate. Fighting back was not much of an option—the ringleader was literally twice my weight. When I tried to fight back, the gang looked at each other with amusement. "Uh oh," they said, "Chucky's getting mad! Did your daddy tell you to stand up to us, Chucky?" The next thing I knew, I was on the floor in a submission hold, surrounded by a chorus of mocking laughter. That was what happened when I resisted. Yet submission didn't work either; it appeased them for a day or perhaps a few minutes or not at all. It was an invitation to further violence. In this difficult situation, I internalized the abusers by taking on their opinion of myself as pathetic and contemptible.

In this case, literally fighting back was futile. My initiatory journey took the form of stepping into the unknown of finding new friends—a frightening prospect in the cacophony and chaos of the junior high cafeteria. Exiting the role of victim doesn't usually mean physical combat or legal combat, though it might. Invariably, it means refusing to comply with violation or humiliation. In real life it could be blocking a caller, getting a restraining order, or simply running away. It cannot be a mere gesture. It must be determined and sustained until the old role no longer beckons.

It is worth noting that none of my abusers were particularly bad people. Nor were those who joined in the laughter, nor those who stood by in disapproving silence. They went on to become solid contributing members of society, good fathers and husbands. There was something in the confluence of our biographies that called them to the role of abuser, enabler, or bystander at that moment. The abuser-victim drama issues a powerful casting call. An abusive spouse may no longer occupy that role in a subsequent marriage. The roles allow each actor to discover—and possibly integrate and transcend—something in themselves. So it is society-wide, as well. What will the functionaries of our abusive, degrading, oppressive system become when the drama ends? Already a lot of them are getting sick of their roles. The victim does the abuser no favor by prolonging the drama.

Earlier I wrote that often the point of courage comes when the pain of submission grows intolerable. The erstwhile victim reaches a breaking point and throws caution to the wind. The abuser may still wield the outward apparatus of power, but no longer does that power have an ally within the victim, who becomes ungovernable. A lot of people are reaching that breaking point now. Powering the aforementioned wave of resistance is a hurricane of fury brewing just offshore of official reality. If you want to get a sense of it, subscribe to the Telegram channel "They Say It's Rare." It displays without comment tweets from vaccine-harmed individuals and their friends and families. Thousands upon thousands of tweets, raw, outraged, and indignant. Most of these people will never comply with vaccination again no matter what the pressure, nor will many of their friends. Perhaps this partly explains low public uptake of boosters. (That and the fact that the first two shots did not deliver the promised rewards of immunity or freedom.)

The drama continues. The bully does not relent at the first sign of resistance. On the soul level, the bully serves his purpose only when he provokes real, sustained courage. As resistance grows, so grows the coercion. We are very nearly at a tipping point. The scale is evenly balanced—so finely, perhaps, that the weight of one person may tip it. Could that person be you? Whatever reasons you have to comply, to stay silent, to keep your head down—and they may be very good reasons indeed—please do not accept the insidious false hope that someone else will take the risk if you do not.

What can one person do? Will it matter if I resist if too many others do not? Five percent of the population can be locked up, locked in, or locked out of society. But 40 percent cannot. Will you resist and risk being one of the 5 percent? Safer to wait and see, isn't it? Safer to wait until after critical mass has been reached, and then join the winning side.

Of all the lies of a controlling power, the key lie is the power-lessness of its victim. That lie is a form of sorcery, coming true to the extent it is believed. All modern people live within a pervasive metaphysical version of that lie. In a Newtonian universe of deterministic forces, indeed it matters little what one person does. It is wholly irrational for the discrete and separate self to be brave, to defy the mob, or to stand up to power. Sure, if lots of people do it, things will change, but you aren't lots of people; you are just one person. So why not let other people do it? Your choice won't much affect theirs.

To refute that logic with logic would require a metaphysical treatise that reclaims self and causality from their Cartesian prison. So I won't use logic. Instead I'll appeal to Logos—the fiery logic of the heart. Something in you knows that your private struggles and the choices of just one person are significant. Furthermore, something in you knows when the time has come to make the choice, to be brave. You can feel the approach of the breaking point. It may feel like, "I've had enough. Enough!" It may be a calm clarity. It may be a leap in the dark. Probably you recognize the moment I'm describing; most of us have gone through some life initiation of this kind, bursting out of a cocoon of fear. In that moment you know something significant has happened. The world looks different. That is because it *is* different.

An abuser, whether a person or a system, offers an opportunity to graduate to a new degree of sovereignty. *We claim by example what a human being is.* When made at risk, such a claim issues forth as a prayer. An intelligence beyond rational understanding responds to that prayer, and reorganizes the world around it. We may experience this as synchronicity, which seems to happen with uncanny frequency just at those moments where one takes a leap in the dark. She leaves the abusive spouse in the dead of night with nowhere to go. Yet she is not reckless, because she knows, *It is time.* She steps out into nothingness and Lo! Something meets her foot. A path invisible from the starting point opens with each step along it.

So it shall be. The world will rearrange itself around the brave choices millions of people are making as they trust the knowledge, *It is time.* If you join us, you will be witness to a most marvelous paradox. The transition to a more beautiful world is a mass awakening into sovereignty, far beyond the doing of any hero, any leader, any individual. Yet you will know that it was you—your choice!—that was the fulcrum of the turning of the age.

Epilogue: A Way Home

As I write these words on February 27, 2022, the pandemic has just ended. It is not over as a disease, but as a social phenomenon. No one declared it over. People are still getting sick. Yet the general agreement that we live in a non-ordinary time of sickness is fast subsiding.

A new succession of crises is calling the public's attention. At this moment it is war in Ukraine. By the time you read this book, it is likely to be something else, perhaps an economic crisis. In all of them we will have the opportunity to exercise the sovereignty into which the coronavirus has initiated us.

During Covid, the public has been subject to highly developed technologies of manipulation and control: the construction of narratives, the censorship of dissent, the fabrication of data, the persecution of dissidents, the control of information, and the circumvention of laws, rights, and freedoms. At the moment most of these have been temporarily lifted, but the authorities, emboldened by experience and precedent, have them at the ready to use again with even more sophistication.

Yet the people have become more sophisticated, too. Many of us will not be so easy to manipulate. The authorities will not easily recover public trust. In times of turmoil and uncertainty, we will no longer look to them to show us the way. Where will we look instead? Those new institutions have yet to be born; therefore they cannot rescue us from the uncertainty, but lay on its other side. Let us pray, at least, that it be so, that no Napoleon will appear to rescue us from the chaos of a revolution devouring itself; that no Hitler will emerge to rescue us from the crisis of sense and meaning that is upon us.

Another path lies before us, a path of healing, peace, forgiveness, flourishing; a beauty way. It is not the only path. It is not the widest path nor the easiest to find among the many radiating out into the future from the crossroads I wrote of in "The Coronation." In the last essay of this collection, "A Path Will Rise to Meet Us," I described just the first step on this path, the step away from the abuser. Many of us have taken it. What next? What now? It is time to build a different kind of future. No one will do it for us. We cannot wait for it to happen. We are here to make it happen.

Buckminster Fuller's most famous statement has become a cliché: "You never change things by fighting the existing reality. To change something, build a new model that makes the existing model obsolete." Usually when words become cliché it is because they carry truth; this is no exception.

But what about when the existing reality seeks to crush the new model that would make it obsolete? The zoning commission crushes the ecovillage. The landowners crush the peasant commune. The pharmaceutical companies crush the alternative therapies. Fuller is not saying never to fight. He's just saying that that isn't how to change things.

Even if we sometimes must fight, we will prevail only if we are fighting *for* something, not just against something. When we fight for rather than against, often we needn't fight much at all. That's because winning no longer defines success. Creating something new defines success, and we are not stuck on fighting as the way to achieve it. We need not crush in turn that which seeks to crush ourselves. We can uphold the beauty of the destination in constant invitation for each and all to join us.

Because I am about to write here of "old" and "new" systems, I want first to establish a spirit of welcome rather than judgment. Today, society is dividing along political fault lines, even to the point of splitting families in two. One side crushing the other is not an acceptable outcome—especially knowing which side is likely to be doing the crushing. Let's uphold an end goal of unity. Some will take a longer road than others to rejoin the rest. In the end, all roads converge upon the Golden Land, where we especially welcome those who wandered the farthest away from it.

Any secret wish that "someday, the other side will regret it," any wish that one's opponents will suffer, reveals a loyalty to something besides healing in the world. Are you willing to welcome the other side into a more beautiful world even if they never admit they were wrong? It is a lot easier to let go of beliefs if you don't face the prospect of your enemies dancing triumphantly over your crumpled ego.

A spirit of generosity infuses Buckminster Fuller's maxim. It doesn't mean never to resist violence or oppression. It asks us to shift our primary orientation toward a goal that includes everyone.

Fuller speaks keenly to our present historical moment. Implacable forces propel us toward a nightmare of techno-medico-totalitarianism, ecological degradation, and extreme economic inequality. Surely we must drop everything else to resist these forces, since if they prevail they will crush the green shoots of any alternative we try to build, right? No. Counterintuitively, it is the perfect time for the green shoots to grow into trees.

The time is right because the old reality is so much less hospitable than it was even a few years ago, making the new models all the more appealing.

As mentioned, my wife, Stella, is a healer. A few weeks ago, a woman brought her son in for treatment of a nervous tic and other health issues. Stella, using light touch and what she calls "resonant attention," felt something amiss in his knees. "What's going on with his knees?" she asked.

"Oh, I forgot to mention, he's been complaining of intense knee pain for years," she said.

Stella proceeded to work on the boy's knees. He has been free of pain ever since. His nervous tic disappeared as well.

Why is it that millions, tens of millions of people flock to alternative practitioners like Stella? Is it because we have mounted a successful assault on the edifice of modern medicine, overpowering it with our own array of controlled, randomized, double-blind, peer-reviewed studies? Have people read our critique and then, exercising their reason, concluded that they'd better leave the system? Of course not. Usually the way it happens is that someone tries alternatives out of curiosity or desperation. The "old reality" wasn't working for them, and they are ready to look for something beyond it. They step outside it, and if they are lucky, find a new model of health care that makes the existing one obsolete. Only then are they open to reading the critiques of the old system, which help them make new sense of the world and assure them that yes, it is okay to step into a new one.

How many stories have we heard of people with chronic conditions going to one specialist after another, taking pain medications and other palliatives, slowly declining to the point of desperation, and then discovering a path to healing totally outside medical reality?

Medicine is one of the most common portals into a new reality, because illness is such a powerful initiator. But there are many others. I remember the first time I saw with my own eyes and felt through my own feet the miraculous power of a water retention landscape to heal land, when I visited the Tamera Ecovillage nine years ago. Until then the possibility was theoretical, something I'd only read about. I didn't *know* it.

One might read any number of critiques of the superficiality and inauthenticity of modern human relating. No critique will have a millionth the power of a direct experience of real intimacy, such as is available through all kinds of modalities (authentic relating, circling, the Human Awareness Institute practices, and so many more).

I could say similar things about birthing and dying, education and farming, sex and money, moving the body, using the mind, using the senses, working in groups, and living in community. Unless the critic is somehow grounded in a new model, the critique will have the energy of a complaint. It will foster despair in the listener. That's one reason why I (as a writer) go silent sometimes. When I lose sight of a more beautiful reality and it becomes theoretical, my words become an empty shell. The animate soul within them has retreated to other quarters.

Animated with a living vision of a new model, critique is not complaint but invitation. It says, "You are not crazy for wanting to leave this reality, because there is a different one that could make it obsolete."

Over many decades, brave and brilliant innovators have developed alternative models of everything I've mentioned and more. I call them Technologies of Reunion. Yet despite their obvious superiority to the "existing reality," they have remained marginal. Their brave, brilliant creators received nowhere near the acclaim they deserved; many of them died poor and reviled. Society instead gave obscene rewards to the highest-functioning overseers and exploiters of the old reality.

It really could not have been otherwise, because the old story had not yet played out to its conclusion. The brave and lonely innovators, some famous in small circles, others totally unknown, will enjoy the gratitude of our descendants as they give thanks to us, their nameless ancestors.

The old story may not end of its own accord, but it certainly has reached a choose-your-own-adventure moment. The inevitable course of events has paused in its momentum, posing the question: Which way shall we turn? The Covid era has given us a preview of how the old story might continue. Many find it unfit for habitation. Not just critique, but misery nudges them out of it. But where to? To leave a familiar harbor to dare stormy seas, one must know of a destination. That is what the margin-workers have prepared.

For many people, the nudge may soon become a rude shove in the form of breakdowns in supply chains, the economy, the health care system, or the educational system. The pandemic has set a process in motion that will outlive the pandemic. When the existing reality stops functioning, new models are all the more attractive. The vacuum at the center pulls in the alternatives from the margins, which take over as the new reality.

The spirit of welcome with which we invite people into a new reality isn't just the gateway—it *is* the new reality. That's because of the close link between welcome and trust. What distinguishes a Technology of Reunion from any other innovation—an AI chip, an mRNA vaccine, a combat robot? Technologies of Reunion reverse the trend toward ever-greater control over matter, the body, and each other. They are based in a kind of trust, trust in the tendency of all things toward wholeness, trust in a deep connection among all beings, trust in an intelligence perfusing all life. Thus they represent a kind of homecoming.

The feeling of homecoming I get from a special farm or community or event or composting toilet is the same I get from a person who loves me without judgment. That is the new model of the human being that makes the old vindictive, judgmental, stingy reality obsolete. In trust that someday each of us will find a way home, we welcome each other to a new reality.

Have you wrestled with despair over the last couple years (or the last couple days), feeling what's happening in the world?

Perhaps you have noticed that despair feels very much like being stranded away from home, never to return. If you are in it now, you will read these words through a veil of cynicism. I won't fight that reality, but I would like to offer a small dose of medicine. It is simply this: Touch your knowledge—which is *already there*, coexisting perhaps with cynicism and despair—that indeed, each of us will find a way home. Recognize that as true; illogical, maybe, but true. Then, even without a map, you will recognize the first step onto the homecoming path. The Queen comes into her queendom, the King into his kingdom, and We the People into democratic sovereignty.

Notes

"Zika and the Mentality of Control"

1. Jay Syrmopoulos, "'It's Not the Zika Virus'—Doctors Expose Monsanto Linked Pesticide as Cause of Birth Defects," The Free Thought Project (website), February 14, 2016, http://thefreethoughtproject .com/doctors-groups-deny-microcephaly-zika-connection-blame -monsanto-linked-pesticide-birth-defects/.

"The Coronation"

1. Ruiyun Li et al., "Substantial Undocumented Infection Facilitates the Rapid Dissemination of Novel Coronavirus (SARS-CoV-2)," *Science* 368, no. 6490, March 16, 2020: 489–93, https://doi.org/10.1126 /science.abb3221.

2. Justin D. Silverman, Nathaniel Hupert, and Alex D. Washburne, "Using Influenza Surveillance Networks to Estimate State-Specific Case Detection Rates and Forecast SARS-CoV-2 Spread in the United States," preprint, medRxiv, April 14, 2020, https://doi.org/10.1101 /2020.04.01.20050542.

3. Eran Bendavid et al., "COVID-19 Antibody Seroprevalence in Santa Clara County, California," preprint, medRxiv, April 30, 2020, https:// doi.org/10.1101/2020.04.14.20062463.

4. Timothy W Russell et al., "Estimating the Infection and Case Fatality Ratio for COVID-19 Using Age-Adjusted Data from the Outbreak on the Diamond Princess Cruise Ship," preprint, medRxiv, March 9, 2020, https://doi.org/10.1101/2020.03.05.20031773.

5. The Food and Agriculture Organization (FAO), *100 Days to Rio +20, 100 Facts: Making the Link between People, Food and the Environment* (Rome: Food and Agriculture Organization of the United Nations, 2012); FAO, IFAD, UNICEF, WFP, and WHO, *The State of Food Security and Nutrition in the World: Transforming Food Systems for Food Security, Improved Nutrition and Affordable Healthy Diets for All*

(Rome: Food and Agriculture Organization of the United Nations, 2021), https://doi.org/10.4060/cb4474en.

6. Lissa Rankin, "Death is No Ending, So Let's Try to Live & Die Well," Lissa Rankin, MD (blog), https://lissarankin.com/death-is-no-ending/.

7. "Coronavirus Will Change the World Permanently. Here's How," *Politico Magazine*, March 19, 2020, https://www.politico.com/news /magazine/2020/03/19/coronavirus-effect-economy-life-society -analysis-covid-135579.

8. Jaime Rosenberg, "The Effects of Chronic Fear on a Person's Health," *The American Journal of Managed Care*, MJH Life Sciences, November 11, 2017, https://www.ajmc.com/view/the-effects-of-chronic -fear-on-a-persons-health.

9. Steven W. Cole et al., "Myeloid Differentiation Architecture of Leukocyte Transcriptome Dynamics in Perceived Social Isolation," *PNAS* 112, no. 49 (2015): 15142–47, http://doi.org/10.1073/pnas .1514249112; Alice G. Walton, "7 Ways Loneliness (And Connectedness) Affect Mental Health," *Forbes*, October 30, 2018, https:// www.forbes.com/sites/alicegwalton/2018/10/30/7-ways-loneliness -and-connectedness-affect-mental-health/; Kate Anderton, "Social Contact Could Play an Important Role in Staving Off Dementia," review of "Association of Social Contact with Dementia and Cognition: 28-Year Follow-Up of the Whitehall II Cohort Study," by A. Sommerlad et al., *PLOS Medicine* 16, no. 8 (2019): e1002862, https:// doi.org/10.1371/journal.pmed.1002862, News-Medical.net, https:// www.news-medical.net/news/20190803/Social-contact-could-play -an-important-role-in-staving-off-dementia.aspx.

10. Lissa Rankin, "The #1 Public Health Issue Doctors Aren't Talking About," filmed July 21, 2016, TEDx Talks (TEDxFargo) video, 19:37, https://www.youtube.com/watch?v=s2hLhWSlOl0.

11. Joseph Stromberg, "The Hygiene Hypothesis: How Being Too Clean Might Be Making Us Sick," Vox, January 28, 2015, https://www.vox .com/2014/6/25/5837892/is-being-too-clean-making-us-sick.

12. Aislinn D. Rowan-Nash et al., "Cross-Domain and Viral Interactions in the Microbiome," *Microbiology and Molecular Biology Reviews* 83, no. 1, (January 2019): https://doi.org/10.1128/MMBR.00044-18.

13. *Report sulle caratteristiche dei pazienti deceduti positivi a COVID-19 in Italia Il presente report è basato sui dati aggiornati al 17 Marzo 2020*, Epidemiology for Public Health, Istituto Superiore di Sanità (Italian National Institute of Health), March 17, 2020, https://www.epicentro .iss.it/coronavirus/bollettino/Report-COVID-2019_17_marzo-v2.pdf.

14. Chris Iliades, "What to Know About NAC Supplements," UHN Daily, January 20, 2021, https://universityhealthnews.com/daily/nutrition/nac-benefits-helps-lung-problems-addictions-autism-bipolar-and-more/; S. De Flora, C. Grassi, and L. Carati, "Attenuation of Influenza-Like Symptomatology and Improvement of Cell-Mediated Immunity with Long-Term N-Acetylcysteine Treatment," *European Respiratory Journal* 10 (April 1997): 1535–41, https://doi.org/10.1183/09031936.97.10071535.
15. Brig Klyce, "Viruses and Other Gene Transfer Mechanisms," Cosmic Ancestry, n.d., https://www.panspermia.org/virus.htm.
16. Lynn Margulis, *Symbiotic Planet*, Basic Books, 1998, 64.

"The Conspiracy Myth"

1. Alleen Brown, "In the Mercenaries' Own Words: Documents Detail TigerSwan Infiltration of Standing Rock," The Intercept, November 15, 2020, https://theintercept.com/2020/11/15/standing-rock-tigerswan-infiltrator-documents/
2. Debora Patta, "'I'm Starving Now': World Faces Unprecedented Hunger Crisis," *CBS News*, May 4, 2020, posted on Yahoo News, https://news.yahoo.com/im-starving-now-world-faces-224051093.html.

"Numb"

1. Liv McNeil, "Numb," YouTube video, 3:22, posted June 18, 2020, www.youtube.com/watch?v=iSkbd6hRkXo.
2. Julianne Holt-Lunstad et al., "Loneliness and Social Isolation as Risk Factors for Mortality: A Meta-Analytic Review," *Sage Journals* 10, no. 2 (March 2015): 227–37, https://doi.org/10.1177/1745691614568352.

"The Banquet of Whiteness"

1. Will Sommer, "Trump's New Favorite COVID Doctor Believes in Alien DNA, Demon Sperm, and Hydroxychloroquine," Daily Beast, July 28, 2020, www.thedailybeast.com/stella-immanuel-trumps-new-covid-doctor-believes-in-alien-dna-demon-sperm-and-hydroxychloroquine.
2. KeithDB, "Why America Fails," Daily Kos, July 30, 2020, http://www.dailykos.com/stories/2020/7/29/1964869/-Why-America-Fails; Dickens Olewe, "Stella Immanuel—The Doctor Behind Unproven Coronavirus Cure Claim," *BBC News*, July 29, 2020, posted by Geo, One Political Plaza, July 29, 2020, http://www.onepoliticalplaza

.com/t-190637-1.html; this article has since been removed from the internet.

3. Qingwei Li et al., "The Role Played by Traditional Chinese Medicine in Preventing and Treating COVID-19 in China," *Frontiers of Medicine* 14 (July 2020): 681–88, https://doi.org/10.1007/s11684-020-0801-x.

4. David Cyranoski, "China Is Promoting Coronavirus Treatments Based on Unproven Traditional Medicines," *Nature*, May 6, 2020, http://doi.org/10.1038/d41586-020-01284-x.

5. Linda Givetash, "China Is Encouraging Herbal Remedies to Treat COVID-19. But Scientists Warn against It," *NBC News*, April 5, 2020, http://www.nbcnews.com/news/world/china-encouraging -herbal-remedies-treat-covid-19-scientists-warn-against-n1173041.

6. Pratik Jakhar, "Covid-19: China Pushes Traditional Remedies amid Outbreak," *BBC News*, June 29, 2020, http://www.bbc.com/news /world-asia-53094603.

7. Jessica Yi Han Aw, Vasoontara Sbirakos Yiengprugsawan, and Cathy Honge Gong, "Utilization of Traditional Chinese Medicine Practitioners in Later Life in Mainland China," *Geriatrics* 4, no. 3 (August 2019): 49, https://doi.org/10.3390/geriatrics4030049.

8. Linda Givetash, "China Is Encouraging Herbal Remedies."

9. Bernard Crutzen, "The Malaria Business: Big Pharma vs Natural Medicine," France 24 English, Camera One Television Zistoires and RTBF Belgian TV, YouTube video, 38:18, posted January 12, 2019, http://www.youtube.com/watch?v=OvC4uSYprU8&t=1s.

10. Bukola Adebayo, "Amid WHO Warnings and with No Proof, Some African Nations Turn to Herbal Tonic to Try to Treat Covid-19," *CNN*, May 15, 2020, http://edition.cnn.com/2020/05/15/africa /madagascar-coronavirus-herbal-remedy-who-intl/index.html.

11. Bayo Akomolafe, "Dear White People," Báyò Akómoláfé (website), June 10, 2016, https://www.bayoakomolafe.net/post/dear -white-people.

12. Charles Eisenstein, *The Ascent of Humanity*, Panenthea Press, 2007, 214–215.

13. P. W. Newacheck, P. P. Budetti, and P. McManus, "Trends in Childhood Disability," *American Journal of Public Health* 74, no. 3 (March 1984): 232–36, https://doi.org/10.2105/ajph.74.3.232; Christina D. Bethell et al., "A National and State Profile of Leading Health Problems and Health Care Quality for US Children: Key Insurance Disparities and Across-State Variations," *Academic Pediatrics* 11, no. 3, suppl. S22–S33 (May 2011): 22–33, https://doi.org/10.1016/j.acap.2010.08.011.

"Life of the Festival"

1. S. Mark Heim, "The End of Scapegoating," in *Study Guides for Patterns of Violence* (Waco, TX: Institute for Faith and Learning at Baylor University, 2016), 20–27, https://www.baylor.edu/content/services/document.php/264317.pdf.
2. Heim, 21–22.
3. René Girard, *Violence and the Sacred*, Continuum Books, 2005, 127. Originally published by Editions Bernard Grasset, Paris, 1972. Trans. Patrick Gregory.
4. Philip Carr-Gomm, "The Eight-Fold Year," Order of Bards, Ovates & Druids (OBOD) website, https://druidry.org/resources/the-eight-fold-year.
5. Girard, 133.
6. Girard, 146.

"Fascism and the Antifestival"

1. Girard, 129.
2. Girard, 31.
3. Girard, 31.

"Mob Morality and the Unvaxxed"

1. Brian K. Smith, "Capital Punishment and Human Sacrifice," *Journal of the American Academy of Religion* 68, no. 1 (March 2000): 3–25.
2. Roberta M. Harding, "Capital Punishment as Human Sacrifice: A Societal Ritual as Depicted in George Eliot's *Adam Bede*," *Buffalo Law Review* 48, no. 1 (Winter 2000): 175–297.
3. Harding, 197.
4. Melinda Wenner Moyer, "Vaccines Are Pushing Pathogens to Evolve," *Quanta Magazine*, May 10, 2018, https://www.quantamagazine.org/vaccines-are-pushing-pathogens-to-evolve-20180510/.
5. Hooman Noorchashm, "WARNING FOR IMMEDIATE CORRECTION—WSJ Editorial Falsehood Re: Susceptibility of COVID-Recovered to Re-Infection," Medium, July 20, 2021, https://noorchashm.medium.com/warning-for-immediate-correction-wsj-editorial-falsehood-re-susceptibility-of-covid-recovered-4d0b0656cdd; David Rosenberg, "Natural Infection vs. Vaccination: Which Gives More Protection?" *Israel National News*, July 13, 2021, https://www.israelnationalnews.com/news/309762.
6. Jean Twenge, "What Psychologists Say About Anti-Vaxxers: They're Raging Narcissists," Daily Beast, February 9, 2015, http://www

.thedailybeast.com/what-psychologists-say-about-anti-vaxxers-theyre
-raging-narcissists; Zachary Petrizzo, "White Nationalist 'Groyper'
Movement Links up with Anti-Vaxxers, Threatens Use of Weapons,"
Salon.com, April 8, 2021, http://www.salon.com/2021/04/08/white
-nationalist-groyper-movement-links-up-with-anti-vaxxers-threatens
-use-of-weapons/; Virginia Heffernan, "Column: Eric Clapton's Not
God, Just Another Vile Anti-Vaxxer," *Los Angeles Times*, July 23, 202,
http://www.latimes.com/opinion/story/2021-07-23/eric-clapton
-vaccination-covid-19-reaction-van-morrison; Jonathan Vanian,
"Russian Disinformation Campaigns Are Trying to Sow Distrust
of COVID Vaccines, Study Finds," *Fortune*, July 23, 2021, https://
fortune.com/2021/07/23/russian-disinformation-campaigns-are
-trying-to-sow-distrust-of-covid-vaccines-study-finds/; Richard Pan,
"Opinion: Anti-Vaccine Extremism Is Akin to Domestic Terrorism,"
Washington Post, February 28, 2021, http://www.washingtonpost.com
/opinions/anti-vaccine-extremism-is-akin-to-domestic-terrorism
/2021/02/26/736aee22-787e-11eb-8115-9ad5e9c02117_story.html.
7. "Top American Doctor: COVID Shots Are 'Obsolete,' Dangerous,
Must Be Shut Down," *The John-Henry Westen Show*, 38:25, Rumble,
July 23, 2021, http://rumble.com/vk8cpw-top-american-doctor
-covid-shots-are-obsolete-dangerous-must-be-shut-down.html.

"The Sacrificial King"

1. Heim, 21.
2. Kathy Frankovic, "Most Americans Now Believe the Coronavirus
Originated from a Laboratory in China," YouGovAmerica, June 3,
2021, http://today.yougov.com/topics/politics/articles-reports
/2021/06/02/most-americans-now-believe-coronavirus-originated-.

"A Temple of This Earth"

1. Heim, 24.
2. Heim, 26.
3. Thich Nhat Hanh, "Call Me by My True Names," *Call Me By My True
Names* (Berkeley, CA: Parallax, 1999).

"A Path Will Rise to Meet Us"

1. "World Medical Association Boss Compares New Strain of
COVID-19 with Ebola," NEWS.am, November 27, 2021, http://
news.am/eng/news/674604.html.

About the Author

Patsy Eisenstein

C harles Eisenstein is a countercultural philosopher, essayist, speaker, and the author of several books, including *Sacred Economics* and *The More Beautiful World Our Hearts Know Is Possible*. He graduated from Yale University with a degree in Mathematics and Philosophy before spending the next decade in Taiwan, where he worked as a Chinese-English translator. He has four children, all boys, and currently lives with his wife in Rhode Island.

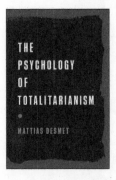

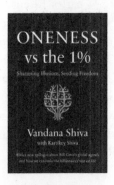